"A most timely, original and necessary additioı
Clare Brooks, *Professor of Education, University of Greenwich,*

"This is a major contribution to the scholarship on expert educational practice and how it is constituted."
Johan Muller, *Emeritus Professor of Curriculum, University of Cape Town, South Africa*

"Jim Hordern's book is essential reading for anyone in professional or vocational education... It is an accessible, insightful and innovative contribution to the sociology of education and curriculum theory."
Professor Leesa Wheelahan, *William G. Davis Chair in Community College Leadership, Ontario Institute for Studies in Education, University of Toronto, Canada*

"This is a rare and welcome book on educational theory and practice. By introducing the idea of different forms of practice for different purposes it will...significantly widen debates about curriculum and pedagogy."
Michael Young, *Emeritus Professor of Sociology of Curriculum, UCL Institute of Education, UK*

RETHINKING KNOWLEDGEABLE PRACTICE IN EDUCATION

The concepts of knowledge and practice are frequently discussed in education – but what is meant by these ideas, and how do they relate to each other? Drawing on recent research, this book breaks new ground to provide novel approaches to conceptualising educational practice, educational judgement and professional knowledge.

This text focuses on the relationship between knowledge and practice in the study of education, developing the notion of 'knowledgeable practice' with the aim of rethinking how we understand the knowledge–practice relation in fields such as professional and vocational education, teaching and curriculum studies. It builds on studies in the sociology of educational knowledge and on theories of expertise and practice which emerge from more philosophical traditions.

By developing a nuanced notion of the relation between knowledge and practice that can serve in the further exploration of policy and practice contexts in education, this book encourages critical engagement with how education is conceptualised in the light of the ongoing and emerging challenges that educators are facing today.

Jim Hordern is Senior Lecturer in the Department of Education, University of Bath, UK and Senior Research Fellow at the Plymouth Institute of Education, University of Plymouth, UK.

FOUNDATIONS AND FUTURES OF EDUCATION

Peter Aggleton, University of New South Wales, Australia
Sally Power, Cardiff University, UK
Michael Reiss, University College London, UK

Foundations and Futures of Education focuses on key emerging issues in education as well as continuing debates within the field. The series is inter-disciplinary, and includes historical, philosophical, sociological, psychological and comparative perspectives on three major themes: the purposes and nature of education; increasing interdisciplinarity within the subject; and the theory-practice divide.

Paying for Education
Debating the Price of Progress
Peter Davies

Education for Sustainable Development in the Postcolonial World
Towards a Transformative Agenda for Africa
Leon Tikly

Paradoxes of Democracy, Leadership and Education
Struggling for Social Justice in the Twenty-first Century
Edited by John Schostak, Matthew Clarke and Linda Hammersley-Fletcher

Learning as Social Practice
Beyond Education as an Individual Enterprise
Edited by Gunther Kress, Staffan Selander, Roger Säljö and Christoph Wulf

Queering Higher Education
Troubling Norms in the Global Knowledge Economy
Louise Morley and Daniel Leyton

Rethinking Knowledgeable Practice in Education
Jim Hordern

For more information about this series, please visit: https://www.routledge.com/Foundations-and-Futures-of-Education/book-series/FFE

RETHINKING KNOWLEDGEABLE PRACTICE IN EDUCATION

Jim Hordern

Routledge
Taylor & Francis Group

LONDON AND NEW YORK

Cover image: © Getty Images

First published 2024
by Routledge
4 Park Square, Milton Park, Abingdon, Oxon OX14 4RN

and by Routledge
605 Third Avenue, New York, NY 10158

Routledge is an imprint of the Taylor & Francis Group, an informa business

British Library Cataloguing-in-Publication Data
A catalogue record for this book is available from the British Library

Library of Congress Cataloging-in-Publication Data
Names: Hordern, Jim, author.
Title: Rethinking knowledgeable practice in education / Jim Hordern.
Description: Abingdon, Oxon ; New York, NY : Routledge, 2024. |
Series: Foundations and futures of education | Includes bibliographical
references and index.
Identifiers: LCCN 2023051493 (print) | LCCN 2023051494 (ebook) |
ISBN 9780367515706 (hardback) | ISBN 9780367515744 (paperback) |
ISBN 9781003054474 (ebook)
Subjects: LCSH: Teaching--Methodology. | Education--Aims and
objectives. | Knowledge, Theory of.
Classification: LCC LB1025.3 .H675 2024 (print) |
LCC LB1025.3 (ebook) | DDC 371.102--dc23/eng/20231129
LC record available at https://lccn.loc.gov/2023051493
LC ebook record available at https://lccn.loc.gov/2023051494

ISBN: 978-0-367-51570-6 (hbk)
ISBN: 978-0-367-51574-4 (pbk)
ISBN: 978-1-003-05447-4 (ebk)

DOI: 10.4324/9781003054474

Typeset in Galliard
by Taylor & Francis Books

CONTENTS

PREFACE

This book focuses on the relationship between knowledge and practice in the study of education, developing the notion of 'knowledgeable practice' with the aim of rethinking how we understand the knowledge–practice relation in fields such as professional and vocational education, teaching and curriculum studies. The book is a culmination of a number of years' reflection on the topic, and builds on studies in the sociology of educational knowledge and on theories of expertise and practice which emerge from more philosophical traditions.

This book has also taken some time to write! This was partly because of the Covid pandemic, which arrived quite soon after the proposal for the book was agreed and work had commenced. The pandemic had an immediate impact on universities in terms of expectations around the balance between teaching and research work, and many of us found ourselves involved with new challenges in terms of teaching, assessment and student support beyond those we had previously faced. This inevitably meant that some longer-term activities, such as writing books, had to take a back seat. Furthermore, the challenges of having primary-school-aged children at home for long periods of time are not to be underestimated. That said, the aftermath of the pandemic, in terms of readjustments to something like a 'normal' way of working, also took toll. It was only about mid-way through 2022 that I started to return to working on this book and to refining its arguments. Hopefully the slightly stop-start nature of the book's construction has not diminished its value or the salience of its arguments.

Overall, I hope the book is useful in terms of progressing a mode of thought that is useful both for critiquing current policy and practice in education and for imagining better educational futures in the interests of individuals, communities and wider society. Those of us who are interested in education are compelled to juggle between the considerations of research, policy and practice. This book attempts, in its own way, to provide a pathway through this and to provoke some further questions for ongoing debate.

ACKNOWLEDGEMENTS

I'd like to first of all express my thanks to my family – Basia, Adam and Daniel – for their support and ongoing entertainment.

A number of people have been particularly supportive and encouraging in terms of my research interests. The late Geoff Whitty was outstanding in his encouragement of my work – it was a privilege to be his colleague at Bath Spa University in the final years of his career. I would like to express particular gratitude to Michael Young, Joe Muller, Leesa Wheelahan, Lorna Unwin, David Guile and my PhD supervisors at Huddersfield – John Craig and Pete Woodcock – who in various ways have been very helpful and supportive along the way. I am grateful also to Christine Eden and Alan Howe for recruiting me to my first lecturing post at Bath Spa University, to James Avis and Bill Esmond for kindly offering me a visiting professorship at the University of Derby, and to Lorna Unwin and David Guile for employing me as a John Adams Research Fellow at the IOE in London soon after completing my PhD. Yael Shalem and Stephanie Allais from Wits University, and their colleagues and students, have showed more interest in my work than most and have provided me with plenty to think about.

Colleagues at various universities and wider organisations also deserve particular thanks for their collegiality and generous research collaboration – not least those who I have worked with on various projects, initiatives, special issues and other publications, including Brian Barrett, Zongyi Deng, Maria Teresa Tatto, Ian Menter, Kendra McMahon, Clare Brooks, Chris Winch, Ursula Hoadley, John Morgan, Andrea Laczik, Kevin Orr, Dan Bishop, Matthias Pilz, Simon McGrath, Anne Parfitt, Catherine Simon, Nick Sorensen, Linda La Velle, Caroline Whiting, Nick Pratt and Pete Kelly. Furthermore, I have greatly appreciated other colleagues for their dialogue on ideas, invitations to participate in activities or suggestions for new directions, not least: Howard Gibson,

Paul McLaughlin, Martin Levinson, Dan Davies, Ye Liu, Jeanne Gamble, Robin Simmons, Gert Biesta, John White, Alison Fuller, Jan Derry, David Lambert, Arthur Chapman, Richard Pountney, Gavin Moodie, Elizabeth Rata, Graham McPhail, Carol Bertram, Alison Kitson, Di Swift, Mike Klassen, Jan Gustafsson Nyckel, John Furlong, Trevor Mutton, Gerald Grace, Mark Priestley, Stephen Billett, James Avis, Mark Addis, Jorg Markowitsch, Olly Newton, Ellen Krogh, Ann-Marie Bathmaker, Volker Wedekind, Stephen Ward, Chris Collier, Darren Garside, Verity Campbell-Barr, Ulrike Hohmann, Chris James, Hugh Lauder, Andrea Abbas, Rita Chawla-Duggan, Jeff Thompson, Tristan Bunnell, Pedro Pineda, Andres Sandoval-Hernandez, Mary Hayden, Graham Nutbrown and Mike Fertig. Graham Gibbs at the University of Huddersfield also deserves special thanks for his teaching on the postgraduate research programme there as I started my PhD in 2008, as do the Sociology Department at the University of Manchester where I completed an undergraduate degree in the 1990s.

Many thanks also to colleagues who I've had the pleasure of working with at Bath Spa, Bath, IOE, London, and Plymouth, and also members of the Editorial Management Committee of the *Journal of Vocational Education and Training*. It would be difficult to list all of them – but I am grateful for their ongoing support and friendship. I'd like also to thank the Society for Educational Studies, the Higher Education Academy, the Gatsby Charitable Foundation and the Edge Foundation for funding various research projects.

PERMISSIONS

The author is grateful to Taylor & Francis for permitting the reuse and revision of the following previously published articles in respect of the preparation of Chapters 6, 7 and 8:

Hordern, J. (2016). Differentiating knowledge, differentiating (occupational) practice. *Journal of Vocational Education and Training, 68*(4), 453–469.

Hordern, J. (2015). Teaching, teacher formation, and specialised professional practice. *European Journal of Teacher Education, 38*(4), 431–444.

Hordern, J. (2022). Powerful knowledge and knowledgeable practice. *Journal of Curriculum Studies, 54*(2), 196–209.

1

INTRODUCTION

The relationship between knowledge and practice (in education)

This book aims to rethink the relationship between educational knowledge and practice in order to cast new light on some important educational debates. The book argues that how we think about 'practice' has a profound impact on how we understand educational activities, responsibilities, the organisation of educational systems, the curriculum and professionalism. Systematic and authoritative educational knowledge (and therefore also knowledgeable activity in education) are only possible if we develop a stronger understanding of practice that is predicated on normativity, mutual accountability and sense of the socio-historical development of the practice. This also includes a deep and robust understanding of the ideas through which any given practice has been shaped. It is argued, nevertheless, that the organisation and ownership of educational practice is continuously contested, and shaped by national and supra-national policy as much as the demands of specific stakeholders in particular contexts.

This book also represents an attempt to further generate a conceptual language about education that cuts across some of the (often inward-facing) debates about education that occur within its specific sub-fields or sub-disciplines (i.e. in teacher education, sociology of education or studies of vocational education). The conceptual outcomes of the book therefore aim to have purchase on educational thinking across phases, fields and sectors, and this is illustrated through chapters that focus on professional and vocational education, the relationship between evidence and practice in education systems, on teacher formation and on curriculum theory. The argument is that in order to progress central debates about education we need to consider the relevance and applicability of educational ideas across the *whole sphere of educational activity*, rather than

DOI: 10.4324/9781003054474-1

remaining concerned only with our particular interests as researchers and educationalists. It is argued that the relationship between knowledge and practice is one such central debate that needs further discussion (hence this book) – with considerable relevance for a range of educational processes and phenomena (e.g. curriculum and pedagogy, teacher education) as much as those which have substantive broader influence on the structure and organisation of education (e.g. educational policy-making).

The aim of this book is to bring some clarity to the debate by advancing criteria by which practices can be *differentiated* so that we can better understand how certain practices allow for the generation of educational knowledge, expertise and sound educational judgement. Key distinctions which will be explored are (i) the differences between 'regulative', 'regularist' and 'normative' theories of practice (Rouse 2007), and (ii) between theories of practice that may seek to encompass all human habitual activity and those that seek to specify more closely the criteria for the development of certain kinds of internal and external goods that might be valuable to communities and society (MacIntyre 2007; Hager 2011). However, the more normative notions of practice (which allow for the generation of systematic expertise, mutual accountability and professional organisation and learning (Rouse 2007; Winch 2010) must nevertheless be better understood sociologically or perhaps socio-epistemically (Muller 2014; Hordern 2018), so that we can more fully grasp the processes by which knowledge and understanding (appropriate to the practice) are evaluated, validated and iterated over time. While knowledge can be systematised, stored and archived independently of the practice in and for which it was generated, it is only through certain types of specialised normative practice that expert knowledge can initially be validated and assured – and later reactivated appropriately to meet new purposes and the demands of fresh contexts (Valleriani 2014; Hordern 2021). Advances in the sociology of educational knowledge must be articulated with better understanding of the conditions through which that knowledge can be continually revised to take account of the demands and purposes of the practice, and thereby provide for fuller and more truthful understandings of the practice to which that knowledge relates. This is what this book aims to elaborate.

Structure of the book

Part I of the book consists of an introduction (Chapter 1), followed by the substantive development of the notion of 'knowledgeable practice' and its relation to the sociology of educational knowledge and educational theory (in Chapters 2, 3, 4 and 5). This part will outline the normative theory of practice (following Rouse 2007) that is the basis for the central claim, contrasting this with other understandings of practice that have often been prevalent in educational research. While practice can be conceptualised in non-normative ways, these conceptualisations are insufficient for theorising how expert practices perpetuate over time. In the second and third chapters of the book the relationship between knowledge, expertise and practice will be articulated, with reference in particular to education. It will be suggested that educational activity is a specialised social activity with a specific societal purpose. Therefore, educational activities require expertise and the generation of educational knowledge, and this in turn requires the development and sustenance of normative educational practice. Drawing on Noddings (2003) Rouse (2007), Winch (2010), Hager (2011) and an article I published earlier (Hordern 2018), Chapters 2 and 3 will sketch out notions of the constituent elements of normative, knowledgeable, educational practice by discussing (i) internal goods and their relationship with external goods in education; (ii) mutual accountability; (iii) practice purpose; (iv) prospectivity; (v) the relationship between propositional, inferential, procedural and acquaintance knowledge; and (vi) how the elements of knowledge outlined in (v) require a normative form of practice for their articulation but also for their continued iteration as a body of knowledge. This will be illustrated through examples from various spheres of education.

Chapter 4 discusses the social and organisational dynamics of practice, bringing in a sense of how practice is constituted through collaborative and individual activity, and examining how processes of legitimation within practices can exclude as well as include, thus drawing attention to a differentiation between those practice characteristics that genuinely promote mutual accountability and the pursuit of the practice purpose, and those that simply seek to build and maintain (conservatively) a community of practice, often to the exclusion of new voices or necessary critique. This entails discussing how the organisation of practice is conceptualised in the sociology of knowledge of Collins (1998), Bernstein (2000), Durkheim (2001) and Eyal (2019), considering issues relating to participation, trust, rituals, and the circulation and exchange of ideas. It also locates these discussions within the overall normative framework of practice indicated by MacIntyre (2007), Rouse (2007) and others, identifying some common positions that resonate across a range of authors, but also identifying some persistent questions. Chapter 5 develops the arguments of a contribution I made to a symposium at the 2018 European Conference on Educational Research (published as Hordern 2019) to examine the relationship between prevalent theories of evidence-informed practice in education and the arguments about knowledgeable practice outlined in Chapters 2–4. It is argued that current understandings of the relationship between knowledge and practice that are particularly salient in Anglophone countries, and increasingly so in European countries, are problematically based around regulative or narrow normative perspectives that do not support the development of systematic educational knowledge or deeper educational understanding amongst teachers and other educational practitioners.

Part II of the book, consisting of Chapters 6–8 and the concluding Chapter 9, focuses in greater depth on how the ideas set out in the first part of the book relate to specific aspects of educational practice, covering a range of educational sectors and professional groups. Chapter 6 will discuss knowledgeable professional and vocational practice, arguing for a view of professional and vocational practice that is centred around a conception of systematic professional and vocational knowledge husbanded by a sense of purpose, and commitments to community and accountability. It will be argued that debates about professional and vocational education have been characterised by (i) a tendency not to differentiate sufficiently between different forms of knowledge and practice and (ii) a lack of a theory which can illustrate how these specific elements can be fruitfully interrelated to support the development of competent and expert vocational practitioners. It is therefore worthwhile to explore how normative and less attenuated theories of practice, as outlined by Rouse (2007), Hager (2011) and others, can be brought together with studies of vocational knowledge and its recontextualisation (previously outlined in Hordern 2016) to sketch a conceptualisation of knowledgeable professional and vocational practice. Chapter 7 revises the arguments that I made previously in Hordern (2015) to focus on what notions of knowledgeable practice mean for teaching and teacher education, with a focus on primary and secondary school contexts, arguing that teaching is a good example of a specialised professional practice for which systematic knowledge distinct to the profession is necessary. It will be argued that the formation of teacher expertise needs further theorisation, and this relies on a better conceptualisation of the relationship between disciplinary (subject) and educational knowledge, accompanied by a notion of teaching as a specialised professional practice that relies on normative characteristics of mutual accountability, internal–external goods, prospectivity and the development of criteria by which the quality of practice can be assessed.

Chapter 8 takes the debate more specifically into curriculum issues, discussing the notion of 'powerful knowledge' and considering how this might be enhanced by the notion of knowledgeable practice, arguing that a normative practice which requires certain forms of knowledgeability is central to how we think about the curriculum, and this incorporates a sense of purpose, accountability and good judgement. This chapter locates the work of Young and Muller on powerful knowledge in the context of a substantive conceptualisation of the relation between knowledge and practice, building on arguments I outlined in Hordern (2022). Making a distinction between the focus of the powerful knowledge authors and a curriculum studies that foregrounds the 'practice turn', it is argued that 'normative practice' can help explicate the specialised activities that make powerful knowledge possible. The idea of normative practice provides a basis for the systematic revisability and specialised communities that are said to underpin powerful knowledge, while also illuminating how teachers recontextualise knowledge and reconcile the role of experience with other types of knowledge in a curriculum. Normative practice offers a basis for 'knowledgeable' purposeful practice which suggests that knowledge is never 'for its own sake', but always in pursuit of something 'at stake', although that which is at stake is always prospective. Furthermore, it is only through generating inclusive and participative forms of (normative) knowledgeable practice that communities can acquire the characteristics that enable knowledge to become meaningful and accessible to all in society without retreating into elitism and obsolescence.

In a brief concluding chapter, the research approach taken in the book is reflected upon, with connections made with the rationale for the book which will be discussed in the next section of this chapter. There is the opportunity also to reflect on the contribution to knowledge and how the ideas presented could be employed moving forward. The chapter briefly elaborates on some implications for the interpretation of knowledgeable practice presented in the book and notes some remaining issues for future deliberation.

Rationale for this book

A book such as this is useful to ongoing debates about knowledge and practice, both in the broader fields of professional knowledge, and with particular relevance to education. There is considerable ongoing discussion about educational knowledge – in debates about the curriculum, teaching, vocational education, and in discussion about the use of evidence in education. There is less discussion about *practice itself*, and implicit assumptions are often made by authors, teachers, policy-makers and the public about what is meant by the term 'practice' and how it might be changed in the light of new policies or evidence about 'what works' in any professional or organisational domain. This book seeks to clarify some of the discussions by relating some arguments about the nature of knowledge which have become salient in educational studies to arguments about the distinctive nature of certain types of practice. In so doing, the book charts a path in which notions of specialisation and educational expertise, and the structure of the study of education itself (see Hordern 2023), can be better understood and located in various educational contexts.

This book contributes to multiple ongoing debates in education studies, including in debates about professional education, as the relationship between knowledge and practice in education remains unresolved. This is despite many ideas current in educational discourse (e.g. evidence-based practice, best practice, theory into practice) relying on assumptions about this relationship. This book attempts to rethink and reimagine the relationship between knowledge and practice through the notion of 'knowledgeable practice', drawing on philosophical and sociological thought on practice and expertise. The core argument suggests that specific forms of normative criterial practice which demonstrate certain social dynamics are a precondition for the development of the forms of educational knowledge that make well-founded educational activity and decision-making in education possible. The second half of the book seeks to demonstrate how this conceptualisation restructures our understanding of educational activity, policies and professional judgement in the fields of professional/vocational education, teaching and curriculum studies.

Underpinning the rationale for the book is a commitment to the idea that both 'truth' and 'truthfulness' are important in debates about educational knowledge and practice, as they are in the broader study of education and indeed in academic work more generally. This is not to take a naïve or simplistic view of truth, but rather to see it as sociologically or socio-historically generated, drawing on an interpretation of the work of Williams (2002) and Young and Muller (2007). Williams identifies in contemporary thought a 'demand for truthfulness' which is often accompanied by 'a pervasive suspicion about truth itself'. He suggests that the 'desire for truthfulness drives a process of criticism which weakens the assurance that there is any secure or unqualifiedly stateable truth' (2002, 1). Such a trajectory of thought can reasonably be said to have had a substantive impact on the social sciences and humanities, and to have had considerable bearing on discussions of knowledge, practice and the theory–practice relation in educational studies (Young and Muller 2007). There are always questions when there are attempts to establish 'the truth', and such questioning seems reasonable when there are well-founded criticisms of the extent to which our views of knowledge (and of education) are influenced by our own backgrounds and interests.

However, Williams, commenting on this situation, asks, 'if you do not really believe in the existence of truth, what is the passion for truthfulness a passion for?' and 'what are you being true to?' (2002, 2). In his book he seeks to find a more reasonable accommodation between truth and truthfulness, to try to grasp how it is possible to balance the 'demand for truthfulness' on a sufficient notion of what 'truth' might be. His arguments rest on a genealogical interpretation of the progress of knowledge and understanding, drawing to an extent on Nietzsche's approach, and therefore acknowledging that our ideas of objectivity are socio-historically constructed. Without some sense, nevertheless, that there is a possibility of establishing truth, notions of truthfulness start to collapse – as there is no lodestone to guide the parameters of the critique and nothing that will satisfy the process of criticism. Young and Muller (2007) discuss how in their view the neglect of a nuanced conception of truth has ultimately undermined much of the (new) sociology of education in the UK, which 'began, in Williams's terms, with a radical commitment to truthfulness' (2007, 176). They suggest that this disciplinary tradition has ultimately 'undermined its own project by its rejection of any idea of truth itself' (Young and Muller 2007, 176). In other words, the exercise of truthfulness has become an industry in itself, and disciplinary excellence has become too closely allied with critique. Following Young and Muller's (2007) argument, it could also be suggested that the sociology of education, and indeed broader policy studies in education, have not been sufficiently concerned with thinking through what education itself is for, or the goods that education provides that are of value in society. We might suggest that in educational research more generally there may be advantages in enhancing reflection on the goods and benefits of educational practice (something more philosophical work on education might see as more properly its domain).

When it comes to professional knowledge (which some elements of educational knowledge might be seen as a version of), then the debate about the character of knowledge and practice, and about the theory–practice relation, requires a nuanced consideration of issues of truth and truthfulness. While it may be possible for some commentators to pursue only critical pursuits and question the necessity for deliberation on 'truth', this is not quite the same for those concerned with professional knowledge or knowledge-in-practice – as there is always concern for a way forward and for judgements that may be made which may have real perceptible impacts on people's lives. In other words, what counts as the truth always matters when we are interested in notions of professional practice and the reasons that professionals may give for their decisions. If we proceed from a point of view that questions the very existence of truth then potentially anything can be justified as a true or better way of proceeding. Apart from anything else, such an approach could give licence to forms of decision-making and judgement which would be unjustifiable, and unacceptable in an inclusive society where we have to trust and rely on each other to go about our daily lives. Without maintaining some sense that something close to a true approximation of events or circumstances (or as true a version as we can possibly get) is possible with appropriate effort, we are also unlikely to be able to exercise truthfulness with any force. Truthfulness relies on a sense that working towards the truth is something worth doing – that there is a point to it. Without this sense of purpose we have only a type of perfunctory activity masquerading as intellectual or professional work. In the case of any form of professional knowledge this isn't good enough, as it evacuates any sense that we must take responsibility for our judgements and decisions as professionals, experts, citizens and fellow human beings.

This book is therefore potentially useful in trying to find a way forward for the relationship between knowledge and practice that acknowledges the considerable literature on the topic, aiming to chart a pathway that can provide a basis for future thinking about professional activity, with a particular emphasis on educational contexts. The spirit in which the book is written is therefore reflective of a commitment to exercise truthfulness while maintaining that there is the potential for a fuller understanding of a 'truer' way of thinking about knowledge and practice, and in particular their relation. Echoing Rouse (2007), whose work distinguishing between types of practice is an important strand of thinking of this book, this process of enquiry recognises that our notions of truth are always 'prospective' and therefore subject to further iteration and development. The approach furthermore also acknowledges that our understanding of knowledge and practice will always be socio-historically and culturally inflected. I hope therefore that this book makes a contribution to a debate that will nevertheless continue to roll on over time, just as it is manifested slightly differently in different jurisdictions and traditions.

References

Bernstein, B. (2000). *Pedagogy, Symbolic Control and Identity*. 2nd edn. New York: Rowman & Littlefield.

Collins, R. (1998). *The Sociology of Philosophies: A global theory of intellectual change*. Cambridge, MA: Belknap.

Durkheim, E. (2001). *The Elementary Forms of Religious Life*. Oxford: Oxford University Press.

Eyal, G. (2019). *The Crisis of Expertise*. Cambridge: Polity Press.

Hager, P. (2011). Refurbishing MacIntyre's account of practice. *Journal of Philosophy of Education*, 45 (3), 545–561.

Hordern, J. (2015). Teaching, teacher formation, and specialised professional practice. *European Journal of Teacher Education*, 38 (4), 431–444.

Hordern, J. (2016). Differentiating knowledge, differentiating (occupational) practice. *Journal of Vocational Education and Training*, 68 (4), 453–469.

Hordern, J. (2018). Educational knowledge: Traditions of inquiry, specialisation and practice. *Pedagogy, Culture & Society*, 26 (4), 577–591.

Hordern, J. (2019). *Knowledge, evidence and the configuration of educational practice*. Paper at symposium on Evidence-Informed Practice at ECER Conference2018 (convenors Tim Cain and Bronwen Maxwell), Bolzano, Italy.

Hordern, J. (2021). Specialised, systematic and powerful knowledge. *London Review of Education*, 19(1), 1–11. https://doi.org/10.14324/LRE.19.1.06.

Hordern, J. (2022). Powerful knowledge and knowledgeable practice. *Journal of Curriculum Studies*, 54(2), 196–209.

Hordern, J. (2023). Educational studies and educational practice: A necessary engagement. *British Journal of Educational Studies*. https://doi.org/10.1080/00071005.2023.2213310.

MacIntyre, A. (2007). *After Virtue: A study in moral theory*. Notre Dame, IN: University of Notre Dame Press.

Muller, J. (2014). Every picture tells a story: Epistemological access and knowledge, *Education as Change* 18 (2), 255–269.

Noddings, N. (2003) Is teaching a practice? *Journal of Philosophy of Education*, 37 (2), 241–251.

Rouse, J. (2007). Social practices and normativity. *Philosophy of the Social Sciences* 37 (1), 46–56.

Valleriani, M. (2014). Introduction: Appropriation and transformation of ancient science. *Nuncius*, 29 (1), 1–8.

Williams, B. (2002). *Truth and Truthfulness: An essay in genealogy*. Princeton, NJ: Princeton University Press.

Winch, C. (2010). *Dimensions of Expertise: A conceptual exploration of vocational knowledge*. London: Continuum.

Young, M. and Muller, J. (2007). Truth and truthfulness in the sociology of educational knowledge. *Theory and Research in Education*, 5 (2), 173–201.

PART I

2

EXAMINING PRACTICE IN EDUCATION

Introduction: conceptualising practice

It seems useful to start by asking how educational practice is conceptualised. In what ways is practice conceived? By whom? And with what outcomes? Discussions of practice abound in educational research, but there is often a lack of precision regarding the substance of discussion – are we clear what 'practice' is when so many authors seem to find its meaning 'unproblematic', and use it 'in very diverse ways'? (Hager 2013, 85). Moreover, there is often a lack of attention in much educational literature to the central questions of who or what shapes (or controls) this practice, and the extent to which it can be changed or transformed by both those involved within the practice, and those outside it. These latter questions start to interrelate with the sociological problematic of the relation between structure and agency, and the institutionalist questions that seek to explain adaptation and isomorphism in human and organisational activity (DiMaggio and Powell 1991). There are also connections with discussions in the humanities and social sciences about the exercise of power through discourse (e. g. via Foucault), or through capital or field positioning (e.g. via Bourdieu, who uses these terms within his theory of practice), and with questions around the development of expertise (Abbott 1988; Winch 2010; Eyal 2019). 'Practice' can be seen as constituted and re-constituted through micro and macro political and sociological dynamics, but the parameters of the reconstitution will depend on how we conceptualise the structure–agency relationship. We cannot just make the assumption that practice is constituted in any particular way in any discussion of educational change and reform. Without an awareness of the varied understandings that can be loaded into 'practice' as a phenomenon we are in danger of being taken off unwittingly into conceptualisations of the world which may be inaccurate, biased or suit particular political agendas (or particular theorists!).

DOI: 10.4324/9781003054474-3

Debates about how we conceptualise 'practice' as a phenomenon may seem remote from much theorisation about education. Nevertheless, it is suggested here that important distinctions about how the term 'practice' is used need to be made, and these have real and substantive implications for how we conceive educational activity, and how this relates to knowledge-ability and expertise. The frequency with which practice is used as a term in the social sciences and the humanities suggests that greater engagement with debates about practice as a concept could be helpful throughout the educational research community. The concept of practice has been elaborated by sociologists, philosophers and organisational theorists in considerable depth, but the parameters of what constitutes a practice vary. In the sections below distinctions are made firstly (i) between more attenuated and less attenuated views of practice, and secondly (ii) between regularist/regulist and normative conceptions. These distinctions, it is suggested, help us differentiate between distinctive perspectives on practice and carry implicit assumptions about the scope of what could constitute a practice.

More attenuated and less attenuated uses of practice

It is clear that there is substantive philosophical and sociological work on the nature of practice, stemming originally from the ancient Greeks. Hager (2013) identifies the 'philosophical lineage' of conceptualisations of practice from the work of Heidegger, Aristotle and Wittgenstein with significant contributions from Dewey, Brandom and Charles Taylor, in addition to sociologists such as Bourdieu and Giddens. This philosophical hinterland is often bound up with ontological and axiological assumptions that reflect the concerns of particular authors who may have been considering how to conceptualise practice as part of a broader intellectual exercise rather than focusing specifically on the term and phenomenon in itself. In the case of Aristotle, for example, the focus may be predominantly on issues of values and life purpose, whereas it could be argued that Giddens and Bourdieu discuss practice only within the context of their broader social theory – practice itself is not necessarily their primary concern. Reflections on how to differentiate between theorisations of practice from philosophical and sociological thought are difficult to find – with attempts to integrate conceptualisations even harder. This leaves us with multiple conceptualisations which may or may not inform contemporary discourse. And yet the term 'practice' is pervasive – and certainly all the more so in discussions of professional knowledge, work and education.

A helpful overview of traditions on 'practice' is provided by Hager, who makes the distinction between 'more attenuated' and 'less attenuated' usages of the term (Hager 2013, 94–96). More attenuated uses tend to be more encompassing, with the view that a very wide range of activity can constitute a practice. More attenuated uses see practice as a 'generic term ... for a whole host of disparate activities' and in circumstances when 'any micro-level human behaviours, activities or even actions' (Hager 2013, 95) are described as practices. There is a great deal of contemporary work in the social, educational and organisational studies fields that appears to be implicitly drawing on these 'more attenuated' conceptualisations and assuming that any activity which occurs habitually could constitute a practice (Nicolini 2013; Lynch et al. 2017). Researchers working with this (often implicitly held and rarely explicated) conceptualisation of practice are often engaged in providing rich description of the micro-level activities of practitioners and 'people's recurrent actions' (Lynch et al. 2017, 3). Such studies might focus on examining a range of habitual or 'routine bodily activities' or exploring what the practice of 'being a competent class student' (Nicolini 2013, 4) entails. In these more attenuated conceptualisations of practice there is considerable scope for engaging with 'non-representational configurations of practice that focus on … materiality, embodiment, situatedness and relationality' (Lynch et al. 2017, 3), which might suggest potential for new forms of descriptive work that theorises the relations between the social and the material.

Those who have worked in some traditions of practice theory have sought to use the notion of practice to develop new lenses to explore the ways in which the social, the material and the physical articulate (Nicolini 2013). Nicolini suggests that most practice theories 'see the world as a seamless assemblage, nexus, or confederation of practices' (2013, 3), and involve the study of 'routine bodily activities' and are concerned with the 'horizon of intelligible action' available to practitioners (2013, 3). Schatzki has focused on the 'shared embodied know how' (2001, 12), 'shared practical understandings' and 'tacit knowledges and presuppositions' (11) that constitute the 'arrays of activity' (11) that can be identified as practices. These approaches can lead to an *all-encompassing* view of practice, and turn attention primarily to the description of either micro-level activities or repetitive action as practice. While such work may have considerable descriptive value in itself, these more attenuated usages offer little guidance on how categories or types of practice can be differentiated from each other, and limited grounds for understanding what holds practices together over time or how they may produce something of value to practitioners or wider society. Why would any habitual activity persist? What drives such activities and how do they change to meet new demands? How do they come to be valued by those who participate in the practice? These questions seem unclear in these more attenuated conceptualisations.

On the other hand, what Hager (2013) terms 'less attenuated' accounts of practice are more selective about what constitutes a practice. The less attenuated account of practice acknowledges the importance of explaining the reasons for the 'interconnectedness' (Hager 2013, 96) of the various elements of a practice, and seeks to address what causes such practices to maintain over a duration and to be considered valuable by practitioners and society. In the less attenuated usage practices are seen as *more than* just individual or collaborative activities that occur habitually, irrespective of how richly such activities can be described and theorised. In such less attenuated versions of practice, criteria for what constitutes a practice are usually developed which require some explanation for how and why interconnected activities hold together over time. MacIntyre's influential conception of practice can be seen as an exemplar of a less-attenuated account of practice, as criteria are established for practices to constitute 'socially established co-operative human activity' with 'standards of excellence' and 'ends and goods' (MacIntyre 2007, 187), as will be discussed further below.

These 'less attenuated' accounts articulate practices as purposeful activities, seeing a concern with purposefulness as a stimulus for the iteration of the practice over time, along with a concern (amongst practitioners) with how performances of the practice can be evaluated using appropriate criteria (Hager 2011; Addis and Winch 2019). While the professions or academic disciplinary areas might be highlighted as archetypal less attenuated practices, MacIntyre's (2007) exemplar practices included fishing, painting and chess, suggesting that what is considered a purposeful activity with widely held standards of excellence should not be confined to specifically institutionalised or regulated activities. The constraints and qualifications stipulated by the less attenuated accounts of practice stand in contrast to the 'more attenuated' accounts, which operate with few parameters and have tended to foreground the contextuality and situatedness of habitual activity as primary characteristics of any practice.

Normative and regularist/regulist notions of practice

An alternative differentiation that is close to that of Hager (2013) is undertaken by Rouse (2007) who argues that conceptualisations of practice can be distinguished between (i) those that are 'regularist' and/or 'regulist' and (ii) those that are 'normative'. On the one hand, those conceptualisations of practice that are 'regularist' or 'regulist' are those in which practice 'participants' are seen to 'repeat the same or similar performances' in a habitual, 'describable' form or to share similar 'presuppositions' about their activities (Rouse 2007, 47). In such conceptualisations, practices are construed as activities which have demonstrable 'regularities' or which are governed by a set of rules (48). Activities that might be habitually undertaken within educational contexts, such as tidying a classroom at the end of a working day or organising an assembly for the school, could be considered as governed by a set of rules established by those working in the setting. In such regulated contexts, practitioners carry out actions in accordance with their shared presuppositions about what is appropriate, whether that be implicit or set out explicitly. Rouse suggests that the regularist and regulist approaches are limited in what they can offer, as they have no clarity on how we might explain how the substance and identity of the practice is 'maintained across multiple iterations' (Rouse 2007, 47). Observations of demonstrable regularity of action or data regarding shared assumptions amongst practitioners cannot in themselves explain how those regularities or presuppositions arise, or, most significantly, how a practice maintains or changes over a period of time. Indeed, it may be the case that such regularities only persist when they are part of a broader more purposeful practice, of which more below. There are noticeable similarities between Rouse's 'regularist' idea and Hager's (2013) 'more attenuated' notion, not least the broad scope of potential activities that could constitute practices in such definitions.

Rouse's (2007) second category, encompassing normative conceptualisations of practice, provide an alternative version that is closely aligned with Hager's (2013) 'less attenuated' accounts. In a normative conception, practices are 'constituted by the mutual accountability of their constituent performances' (2007, 48), asserting that practices only develop where there are ongoing streams of interactions/actions that are undertaken in response to other related actions. The interrelatedness of actions within a practice enables processes of 'holding to account' to emerge by which actions can be evaluated according to some notion of 'appropriateness' that constitutes the essence of the practice (Rouse 2007, 48). Questions are therefore asked regarding whether an interaction seems 'appropriate' in the context of previous and other current interactions? Does a particular action or judgement make sense in the context of the practice, or seem somehow 'out of tune' with its essence? Each 'performance' or interaction that is recognised as part of the practice thus has particular resonance when seen in terms of its relations to other related performances or interactions.

Examples of such normativity in action can be seen in educational contexts. For example, a team of educational researchers deciding on new steps for their investigative inquiries should have a grasp of how various potential courses of action would relate to previous research activities in the field, and therefore be capable of perceiving what any judgement regarding a course of action might lead to. Once any course of action is under way (for example a new round of fieldwork or the use of a new methodology) the researchers can collectively hold the decision to pursue such an action to account in the light of their collective expertise on this and former processes of enquiry, drawing on their collective grasp of previous practice. A similar example can be sketched for construction managers or engineers deciding on a course of action regarding a new project, which might be the renovation of a building or the construction of a new bridge or dam. Again, courses of action can be considered against previous performances of the practice, and potential innovations scrutinised against the existing pattern of interactivity between decisions and their consequences in the field. Decisions, and the practitioners making them, are therefore accountable to the practice and its criteria of appropriate performance.

This interrelationship between mutually accountable activities also sketches a perceptible boundary to the practice: where an activity does not resonate with the stream of responses to previous activities it is not constitutive of the practice. Practice normativity is thus constituted through the nuanced relations between actions which have a bearing on each other (Rouse 2007, 49), which collectively shape the identity of a practice and provide it with a history, a present and a potential future. For those who have sufficient grasp of any given practice each interaction associated with that practice will have special resonance, whereas those not initiated in the practice will not be capable of fully interpreting the meaning of practice activity or may need assistance with the interpretation. This is not to say that the boundary to the practice is impermeable – it may be the case that the practice needs to adjust to new contemporary challenges. In such a situation a new activity may need to be developed or absorbed into the practice, brought through or across the boundary so that it can be incorporated within the framework of existing activities, perhaps causing these to iterate and adapt in turn. The practice thus may be in a state of continual adaptation and change, while maintaining true to its purpose and tradition.

In a normative practice, the 'mutual accountability' of activities can only arise when there is something 'at stake' or 'at issue' which provides a reason for the activities to develop in relation to each other (Rouse 2007, 51). The activities are collectively orientated towards some general aim or purpose, which may only be partially defined or agreed. This is inextricable from a sense that 'the definite resolution' of issues is 'always prospective' (51), and thus there is always the potential for practical improvement or greater insight, in the search for ways to achieve the practice purpose. What Rouse (2007) calls 'prospectivity', or the sense that the pursuit of whatever is at stake is never settled, provides the impetus for practitioners to constantly iterate the practice – to continue discussions, debates, trials and innovations. Furthermore, the nature of what is at stake (in other words the definition of the purpose of the practice) may itself adapt as circumstances change.

A degree of special understanding of the practice will develop amongst those practitioners that engage in the practice over long periods of time, through the related interactions and collective ongoing interpretation of and engagement with the 'issue' that is at stake. Seasoned practitioners will gain a sense of what are appropriate practice interactions, and learn how to apply implicit criteria for assessing potential contributions to the practice, forming the 'appropriateness' by which the 'holding to account' takes place. These criteria may well become more explicit and consensually agreed amongst groups of practitioners over time, defining what is or is not appropriate performance of the practice (Addis and Winch 2019). In terms of new potential activities, these can be weighed against the criteria held by practitioners as defining the qualitative character of the practice.

Standards of Excellence

MacIntyre's (2007) work provides a template for how the criteria of 'appropriate' performance of the practice can be understood, by outlining the notion of 'standards of excellence', by which a practice can be defined and through which practice activity can be evaluated. Such standards are generated through collective understanding of what MacIntyre (2007) calls 'goods internal to the practice', which include both the practitioner's 'excellence in performance' (2007, 189) and the intangible or tangible outcome (which may or may not be a material product) of the practice. Thus, experience both of the process of agriculture and understanding of the outcome of an agricultural process (for example the production of food) are necessary for the identification and ongoing iteration of appropriate standards of excellence. MacIntyre also suggests that practices generate the 'goods of communities in and through which the goods of individual lives are characteristically achieved', therefore claiming that nestled within each practice are the processes of 'shared making and sustaining' which achieve the 'common good' (MacIntyre 1994, 288). The shared making and sustaining found in practices will thus tangibly or intangibly generate socially beneficial outcomes. It is important to note that MacIntyre's definition of a practice is wide-ranging, and includes 'performance arts', 'productive professions or crafts' including 'architecture or weaving', technical disciplines such as 'navigation and military strategy' and academic disciplines such as 'physics and history' (Dunne 2005, 365). These practices operate in diverse ways, and lead to a range of intangible and tangible outcomes, to generate aspects of the 'common good'.

Nevertheless, it would only be reasonable to ask searching questions of this idea of practice. It is important to consider who sets the standards of excellence, and who would decide the criteria by which expressions of the practice would be judged and evaluated. What would count as the 'common good' and how widely should the 'shared making and sustaining' extend? MacIntyre's notion of practice could also be seen as a relatively conservative approach which resists change. Once the practice tradition is embedded, and powerful individuals within the practice are involved in setting the standards of excellence, it may be difficult to adapt these to new requirements emerging from social, economic, technological or environmental change. As Dunne remarks, the 'history' of a practice 'can also enlighten us about how practices are complicit in the circulation of power and the perpetuation of privilege, alerting us to the ease with which allegedly internal considerations can legitimate or disguise hierarchy' (2005, 370). Hager (2011), while having sympathy with elements of MacIntyre's conception, also notes that MacIntyre tends to concentrate his examples on games (such as chess) and would benefit from a more extensive consideration of the outcomes of practice and the relation between internal and 'external goods' (such as property, money, fame). There is also the issue of who might be considered a practitioner if we follow MacIntyre's conception and consider how straightforward it might be for a newcomer to be admitted into the practice. To what extent could the practice iterate and accommodate new potential participants? And what would be needed to support these practitioners to engage with the practice and to provide for full inclusion and participation?

Dunne (2005), working within the neo-Aristotelian framework also occupied by MacIntyre, defines practice as something that 'can succeed or fail in being true to its own proper purpose', highlighting also the probability that internal goods are constantly at risk of being 'subverted by external factors' (pp. 367–8). To a greater extent than other authors Dunne (2005) highlights the extent to which commitment to that which is 'at stake' (Rouse 2007) is central to the ongoing survival of the practice. Drawing closely on MacIntyre he notes that practice 'remains alive only so long as' practitioners 'remain committed to sustaining – and creatively developing and extending – its internal goods and its proper standards of excellence' (Dunne 2005, 368). A risk Dunne emphasises, echoing MacIntyre's discussion of external goods, is that external factors (such as the pursuit of financial rewards or status) can make practice 'instrumental to the point that violation of its internal fabric' (369) eventuates, thus suggesting that there must be sufficient internal strength, organisation and clarity of purpose in the practice to mitigate against the increasing dominance of external concerns. This is not to say that Dunne (2005) or MacIntyre (2007) deny that 'external goods' exist as part of a viable durable practice – rather, they make the point that when 'external' ambitions start to dominate the practice then the 'internal fabric' is at risk of collapsing.

The clarity of purpose regarding the practice purpose or 'telos' is closely related to other aspects of the practice activity. Dunne (2005) notes that 'a practice can indeed be seriously subverted or derailed by weakness or failure in its institutional or educational arrangements' (2005, 370), drawing attention to the significance of processes of apprenticeship and the formation of new practitioners – and how the practicalities and logistics of such processes remain important. Nevertheless, whatever the institutional and logistical challenges faced by a practice, such 'weaknesses or failures can be understood or even acknowledged – let alone effectively addressed – only if there is clarity about the practice itself' (Dunne 2005, 370). Dunne therefore turns our attention back to the process of establishing definitions of the standards of excellence that are appropriate to the purpose of the practice and ensuring that internal goods are realisable. This requires certain types of careful management of practice processes, including ensuring the committed and engaged participation of practitioners, and the welcoming of new practitioners to the practice to contribute to maintaining standards of excellence.

In the work of Dunne (2003, 2005) and Noddings (2003), and in some of my own work (Hordern 2021) and with others (Hordern, Muller and Deng 2021), the case has been made that it is important to challenge MacIntyre's scepticism about the distinctiveness of educational practice. From the point of view of a book that is concerned with conceptualisations of the relation between knowledge and practice across a wide range of educational activity, it is important to consider the parameters of this debate about educational practice, and it is to this which we now turn.

Can education be considered a normative practice?

There has been some debate as to whether education or teaching can be considered normative practices, in Rouse's (2007) terms, or can be considered consistent with what MacIntyre considers to be a practice. It is firstly useful to note that MacIntyre did not consider teaching to be a practice, but rather an 'ingredient in every practice' (MacIntyre and Dunne 2002, 8). However, in dialogue with MacIntyre, Dunne disagreed with this, claiming that teaching has (in itself) its 'own specific goods ... and standards of excellence', and that 'the excellence of teachers is extended through greater realisations of excellence in their students' (MacIntyre and Dunne 2002, 7). Moreover, drawing on the distinction that MacIntyre makes between internal and 'external goods' (which include 'wealth, social status' and 'a measure of power and influence'; MacIntyre 2007, 189), Dunne suggests that excessive focus on the external goods provided by education (e.g. 'test scores or access to occupational pathways leading to high income or status') 'threatens the reliable achievement of its internal goods' (MacIntyre and Dunne 2002, 7). The balance between the internal and the external is significant. We might argue that the external goods obtained through education may 'accrue from accomplishment' in terms of achieving standards of educational excellence and gaining qualifications or other marks of distinction. Nevertheless, the 'practice can be made instrumental' if it (the practice) is enacted in ways that simply 'maximise the external goods' (Dunne 2005, 369) while neglecting the other purposes. External goods, in education as in other practices, become problematic when they are seen as the overwhelming raison d'être of the practice.

Taking a similar line of reasoning to Dunne, Noddings (2003) argues that teaching is a 'relational practice' (241), foregrounding the idea that teaching possesses internal goods connected to the growth and development of students. Noddings appeals to the values that teachers hold, arguing that they seek to 'make a difference in the lives of the students' (247), and that they 'accept some responsibility for the development of students as whole persons' (249). Noddings (2003) suggests that the foremost internal good is 'the development of whole persons' (250), in addition to a subset of goods such as 'intellectual enthusiasm' and the 'challenge and satisfaction shared ... by engaging in new material' (249), and the 'establishing and maintaining relations of care and trust' (250). All of these goods collectively co-constitute the 'distinctive criteria of internal excellence' (251), which could be said to define forms of teaching and educational activity. Dunne (2005) perceives that education has some similarity with politics, in that both can be seen as 'master practices' with concern for the realisation of 'the human good' through community participation *and* 'by individuals as the good of their individual lives' (p. 370). Thus for Dunne (2005) the internal substance of education is interwoven with broader societal benefits: education fosters individual capability and regenerates 'the social'; the private and the public interrelate and are co-dependent. The consequences of educational activity, in terms of individuals and groups with a degree of understanding of the world around them and their potential contribution, have value and benefit to all in society. While the common goods of education may not always be immediately tangible (or measurable), they are inseparable from the practice of education.

In order to fully grasp what constitutes educational practice, if we follow Rouse's (2007) normative conception, we need to consider what really is 'at stake' or 'at issue' in education. It may also be that different stakeholders, for example governments, employers or teachers' organisations, make various claims as to what the primary purposes of education are. Some may claim that an education system or an institution such as a university or a school has multiple purposes, without necessarily considering the weighting and prioritisation of purposes. However, a closer look may reveal that these purposes are contradictory or in conflict, as we might see if educational systems are said to have a role in supporting economic growth or the production of job-ready young people simultaneously to supporting individual formation or social solidarity (Hordern, Muller and Deng 2021). Amongst educationalists a primary purpose of educational practice might be construed as the holistic pedagogical formation of the individual within society, which we can see echoed in much European educational thought (Hopmann 2007; Deng 2020). However, the notion of formation *within society* suggests that how the formation of the individual is conceptualised is likely to be shaped by the socio-historical context in which that formation takes place (Alexander 2001). Furthermore, because of the diversity of educational thought and research there are likely to be ongoing debates and differing perspectives on the combination of educational experiences and activities that are suitable for individual formation, and on the role of education in the delicate relationship between social stability and social change and transformation.

By ruminating on educational purposes, and collectively defining what is 'at stake' in educational practice, practitioners are thereby defining what is 'education' and what isn't. It may be possible to establish a (permeable and constantly changing) boundary around what constitutes educational practice, even if that boundary is only held within the minds of practitioners (and others who can recognise the nature of the practice through their own experience of it). The consequence would be that some activities are clearly 'educational' and some are not, and those who are sufficiently engaged with the practice acquire the capacity to make judgements on what is really educational, and how best to act in educational contexts to achieve the purposes of the practice. There is a role here for standards of excellence (MacIntyre 2007), and a set of explicitly or tacitly held criteria by which judgements in educational contexts can be evaluated (Addis and Winch 2019). It seems reasonable to argue that those who are concerned with educational practice, including policy-makers or leaders within educational systems, should be sufficiently conversant with the collective view of what is 'at stake' in educational practice, in order to make appropriate decisions and propose new strategies in relation to educational activity.

The notion of some form of boundary around what constitutes educational practice does not necessarily deny that there will be some whose experience *within* the boundary may be limited or even non-existent. Attending an educational institution does provide some experience of educational practice, but without taking on particular kinds of educational roles (such as a teacher, mentor, coach or assistant practitioner of some kind) you are unlikely to stay sufficiently within this boundary to be able to make appropriate judgements regarding educational matters. Without an ongoing participation in educational practice you are likely to have a limited understanding of how performances of the practice are mutually accountable to each other, or how the practice is changing over time in response to new demands or interpretations of what is 'at stake'. Nevertheless, it may be possible for those beyond the boundary to measure aspects of the practice through the collection of data focused on what may be considered important to governments, employers or others, some of which might be considered 'external goods' in MacIntyre's (2007) terminology.

Various types of evaluation or analysis of the practice may also be possible for those without sufficient grasp of the 'at stake' issues of educational practice. It may well be problematic, however, if the views of those with limited participation in the practice take precedence over the insights of those with substantial direct acquaintance with the practice, specifically in terms of identifying what is appropriate performance of the practice and determining standards of excellence or criteria for evaluation. To sustain the development of internal goods and the focus on issues at stake requires ongoing deep engagement with the practice and its normative constraints. This therefore suggests that any research or analysis of educational practice necessitates a commitment to the issues that are at stake and to understanding why judgements are made in relation to those issues, and determinations which somehow respond to previous decisions made within the practice itself. Fuller participation in educational practice may also involve acquaintance with relevant traditions, rituals and customs (as will be noted in Chapter 4), so that an informed perspective can be taken on how these customs may need to be challenged and reformed in the face of new challenges. The boundary to any practice remains permeable and open to change, but decisions about changes would need to involve a re-engagement with the purposes of the practice and its standards of excellence, otherwise the essence of the practice itself is lost.

It therefore seems reasonable to conclude that a sound case can be made for seeing education as a type of knowledgeable normative practice in its own right. We will turn to issues of educational knowledge in the next chapter to start exploring what that knowledge might consist of, and how it might be related to practice. However, in advance of this it is just worth briefly summarising some key aspects of the argument so far regarding a reasonable definition of a practice that is normative and characterised by specialised knowledge, particularly in so far as this relates to educational practice. We might therefore suggest that a viable normative practice requires, drawing particularly on Rouse (2007), MacIntyre (2007), Dunne (2005) and Noddings (2003):

i   A purpose, telos or that something is 'at stake' that is shared amongst participants in the practice: a shared understanding of the purpose of the practice.
ii   A notion of prospectivity – no debate about achieving a purpose is ever fully settled, and the practice may need to rethink its processes in the context of changing demands and requirements.
iii   A notion that performances of the practice are somehow 'mutually constitutive' of the practice. In other words, contributions to the practice must somehow make sense in the context of the existing practice, even if the practice is constantly iterating and can potentially be transformed (in terms of its activities and processes) by new contributions.
iv   Clarity about and commitment to internal goods and the standards of excellence that these internal goods might be assessed by.
v   Some form of organisation and processes that sustain the commitment of participants and enable the induction and support of new participants, so that the practice sustains over time.

Over the course of this book, as we engage with different contexts in which notions of knowledgeable normative practice appear relevant (e.g. schoolteaching, professional and vocational education and curriculum theory), we will be able to consider how these criteria (or set of requirements for the definition of normative practice) can be realised.

References

Abbott, A. (1988). *The System of Professions: An essay on the division of expert labour.* Chicago: University of Chicago Press.

Addis, M. and Winch, C. (2019). Introduction. In M. Addis and C. Winch (eds) *Education and Expertise.* Chichester: Wiley, pp.1–20.

Alexander, R. (2001). *Culture and Pedagogy: International comparisons in primary education.* Oxford: Blackwell.

Deng, Z. (2020). *Knowledge, Content, Curriculum and Didaktik: Beyond social realism.* Abingdon: Routledge.

DiMaggio and Powell, W.W. (1991) (eds). *The New Institutionalism in Organizational Analysis.* Chicago: University of Chicago Press.

Dunne, J. (2003). Arguing for teaching as a practice: A reply to Alasdair MacIntyre. *Journal of Philosophy of Education,* 37 (2), 353–369.

Dunne, J. (2005). An intricate fabric: Understanding the rationality of practice. *Pedagogy, Culture and Society,* 13 (3), 367–390.

Eyal, G. (2019). *The Crisis of Expertise*. Cambridge: Polity Press.

Hager, P. (2011). Refurbishing MacIntyre's account of practice. *Journal of Philosophy of Education*, 45 (3), 545–561.

Hager, P. (2013). Practice as a key idea in understanding work-based learning. In P. Gibbs (ed.). *Learning, Work and Practice: New Understandings*. Dordrecht: Springer, pp. 85–103.

Hopmann, S. (2007). Restrained teaching: The common core of Didaktik. *European Educational Research Journal*, 6 (1), 109–124.

Hordern, J. (2021) Why close to practice is not enough: Neglecting practice in educational research, *British Educational Research Journal*, 47 (6), 1451–1465.

Hordern, J., Muller, J. and Deng, Z. (2021). Towards powerful educational knowledge? Addressing the challenges facing educational foundations, curriculum theory and Didaktik, *Journal of Curriculum Studies*, 53(2), 143–152.

Lynch, J., Rolands, J., Gale, T. and Skourdoumbis, A. (eds) (2017) *Practice Theory and Education: Diffractive readings in professional practice*. London: Routledge.

MacIntyre, A. (1994). A partial response to my critics. In J. Horton and S. Mendus (eds) *After MacIntyre: Critical perspectives on the work of Alasdair MacIntyre*. Cambridge: Polity, pp. 283–304.

MacIntyre, A. (2007). *After Virtue: A study in moral theory*. Notre Dame, IN: University of Notre Dame Press.

MacIntyre, A. and Dunne, J. (2002). Alasdair MacIntyre on education: In dialogue with Joseph Dunne. *Journal of Philosophy of Education*, 36 (1), 1–19.

Nicolini, D. (2013). *Practice Theory, Work and Organisation: An introduction*. Oxford: Oxford University Press.

Noddings, N. (2003). Is teaching a practice? *Journal of Philosophy of Education*, 37 (2), 241–251.

Rouse, J. (2007). Social practices and normativity. *Philosophy of the Social Sciences*, 37 (1), 46–56.

Winch, C. (2010). *Dimensions of Expertise: A conceptual exploration of vocational knowledge*. London: Continuum.

3

EDUCATIONAL KNOWLEDGE AND ITS RELATION TO PRACTICE

Introduction

This chapter aims to provide a framework for unpacking the nature of educational knowledge through a differentiated understanding of knowledge and practice, drawing on elements of the work of Durkheim, Bernstein, Young and Muller, and from this explore connections with notions of professional knowledge and expertise (in particular the work of Winch 2010) and the notions of normative practice discussed in the earlier chapter. This proceeds through a consideration of criteria that can be employed to differentiate between what Furlong and Whitty (2017) call educational knowledge traditions, with the aim of advancing the process of distinguishing between approaches to educational thought. Via a focus on the *socio-epistemic* character of educational knowledge and the much-debated relation between 'theory' and practice, and with a reflection on the character of practice in educational contexts, we can seek to establish some parameters within which judgements about educational knowledge can be made. The work of Bernstein on knowledge structures and the broader sociology of educational knowledge is the basis here for differentiating between knowledge (and to some extent practice), in a similar vein to Furlong and Whitty (2017) and my own contribution to Whitty and Furlong's book (Hordern 2017).

However, while acknowledging the insights of Furlong and Whitty's approach, the relationship between specialised knowledge and practice is placed at the centre of the analysis here to better understand the rationale for particular processes of educational knowledge production and how they inform decisions within education systems. Traditions of educational knowledge production can potentially be differentiated depending on the

DOI: 10.4324/9781003054474-4

extent to which they recognise specialised educational knowledge (i.e. knowledge concerned with educational problematics that speak to 'at stake' issues in educational practice). This capacity to recognise specialised *educational* knowledge is related to a conceptualisation of educational practice as a normative activity (as noted in Chapter 2) for which specialised knowledge is necessary.

Unresolved tensions in educational knowledge are often at the heart of debate about the future of education (James 2012; Furlong 2013), underpinning much of what is contestable in educational studies. Various authors over the last twenty years have focused on the nature of knowledge in analysis of curriculum policy and educational reform, including Young and Muller (2014, 2016) and other social realist authors (Barrett and Rata 2015), while others (for example Alderson 2020) have challenged aspects of this project and noted how the interpretations of the work of social realist authors have informed educational policy. Arguments about how educational problems are framed and solutions determined often return to questions of how knowledge validity is determined, and by whom. A relativist view might frame these questions as being primarily about tensions between differing interest groups seeking to define what counts as 'knowledge', while social realism seeks opportunities to differentiate knowledge claims on the basis of commitments both to 'truth' and to 'truthfulness' (Young and Muller 2007). It can be argued that questions of educational value are increasingly marginalised by the push towards empiricism and 'what works' in research design (Hammersley 2005; Biesta 2007; Hordern, Muller and Deng 2021), while there is also longstanding scepticism about whether academic researchers are in a position to make valid claims about educational practice.

Simultaneously, some governments have sought to influence the processes by which educational knowledge is recognised by the academic community, condemning academic educational research for its irrelevance, politicisation or backwardness, as Brian Barrett and I discussed in (Barrett and Hordern 2021). In England, for example, the government has explicitly backed a preferred arbiter of 'valid' educational research (the Education Endowment Foundation (EEF) and a 'what works' movement) which is charged with 'improving and spreading the evidence on what works in education' (DfE 2016, 13). The EEF is responsible for identifying and producing educational knowledge according to specific methods and to meet specific policy objectives, and then disseminating that as a form of official knowledge to schools, thereby implicitly discouraging educational practitioners from exploring other forms of disciplinary educational knowledge. The most recent policy moves in teacher education in England, in particular the development of the 'ITT Core content framework', which is authorised with input from the knowledge selections of the EEF, is a further step in a tightening grip over what counts as educational knowledge (see my paper with Clare Brooks for a further discussion: Hordern and Brooks 2023).

Bernstein, Durkheim and a socio-epistemic approach to the analysis of educational knowledge

Bernstein's (1999, 2000) work, and that influenced by Bernstein (i.e. Beck and Young 2005; Muller 2009; Young and Muller 2016) provides a framework for differentiating between types of knowledge structures and the socio-epistemic processes through which knowledge is produced and revised. While it can be helpful to clearly separate the sociological dimensions of knowledge production from its epistemic character, Bernstein's work and its development by those involved with social realism (i.e. Young and Muller 2016) sees the social and epistemic as inextricable, in that there is an interdependency between knowledge structure and the social processes through which that knowledge is shaped (Muller 2009). The principal origin of this claim is in Durkheim's (2001) elementary forms of religious life, in which Durkheim identifies the division between the 'sacred' and the 'profane' as characteristic of all societies, and that contemporary (European) society is in the process of substituting science for religion as the source of what is considered sacred (or specialised) knowledge. Durkheim describes 'sacred' forms of knowledge as 'collective representations' that have a special or specialised character – they are constructed through the 'work of society' and are 'rich with its experience', providing an 'intellectual realm' that is nevertheless 'subjected to an indefinitely repeated test' as concepts are verified through the engagement of those that 'adhere' to them (2001, 331–3). Sacred or what might be better described contemporaneously as 'specialised' knowledge is made possible through specific forms (or practice) of 'sociality' that provide for ongoing iteration, refinement and adaptation in the light of new realisations, findings or insights (Durkheim 2001; Young and Muller 2016).

Bernstein built upon Durkheim's differentiation between the sacred and the profane through his description of vertical discourse as 'specialised symbolic structures of explicit knowledge' (1999, 161) (as an outline of the sacred), and then further differentiated between 'hierarchical' and 'horizontal/seg-mented' knowledge structures within this specialised discourse. Vertical discourses of specialised knowledge are products of certain social relations which seek to sustain the knowledge itself 'in an ongoing process in extended time' (Bernstein 1999, 161). In horizontal or 'everyday' discourse, however, profane 'repertoires' and 'strategies' born of individual experience are circulated and exchanged to meet specific individual or group objectives (159–160), and are 'exhausted in the context of enactment' (161). Nevertheless, the boundaries between the sacred/vertical/specialised and the profane/horizontal/non-specialised are not fixed indefinitely. Instead, they tend to have a degree of permeability and alter over time, in that notions that have an origin in everyday or contextual activities (i.e. horizontal discourse) can potentially demonstrate their wider relevance and applicability, engaging with the claims and collective representations of specialised knowledge and potentially contributing to that specialised knowledge in time (Muller 2014). On the other hand, some notions that may be considered 'specialised' in one period may later become disputed and discredited and therefore no longer meet the conditions to be identified as specialised knowledge. Ideally, such knowledge would then be removed from the category of 'specialised' and considered non-specialised or become recategorised as 'non-specialised', perhaps retaining some specific relevance only in certain situations.

The sacred (or specialised) and profane (non-specialised), as represented also in Bernstein's vertical and horizontal discourse, can therefore be differentiated by unpacking the socio-epistemic processes that constitute certain forms of specialisation, and the form of practice that gives rise to such processes. Muller (2014) highlights the importance of Winch (2010), suggesting that Bernstein's discourses should be seen as more than just piles of propositional knowledge or conceptual structures. Instead, the vertical discourse of specialised knowledge can be construed as consisting of propositional knowledge held together through inferential relations that provide for meaning. As Winch (2010) argues, inferential and procedural know-how is necessary for related propositions to form a meaningful body of knowledge, and to enable that body of knowledge to continue to iterate as new claims are formulated and put forward. Each specialised knowledge discourse is maintained through specialised procedural processes enacted by communities responsible for husbanding this knowledge, with such processes aiming to refine the overall meaning and purchase of the knowledge in respect of the object of its inquiry. The procedures will encourage new claims to knowledge to be located in respect of the existing knowledge base and will make clear the significance of the new knowledge for the community. Arguably, as Winch (2010) suggests, some types of acquaintance knowledge are also important elements of this specialised knowledge – it is not enough just to 'know that' and 'know how', as some forms of experience of undertaking activities relevant to the specialised knowledge may well be necessary. This starts to open up the possibility that engaging in certain forms of practice through interaction with others and relevant experience becomes integral to engaging successfully with specialised knowledge (as will be discussed in more depth in Chapter 8).

Whitty and Furlong's educational knowledge traditions

Discussions around educational knowledge are heavily influenced by policy contexts and national traditions of educational enquiry. Whitty and Furlong's (2017) comparative study of educational knowledge traditions, cognisant of the political and socio-historical context of educational knowledge, provides a useful starting point for differentiating between knowledge form and purpose in education across national contexts. In their introductory chapter Furlong and Whitty (2017) identify twelve knowledge traditions, categorising them in terms of the 'academic', the 'practical' and the 'integrated', drawing on

Bernstein's (2000) work to unpack the different structures and purposes of educational knowledge. They proceed also to differentiate between 'objective' and 'normative' concerns in the production of knowledge, or in other words the production of knowledge that is 'contestable through accepted protocols within particular epistemic communities' and processes that are ingrained with an 'explicit (or at least clearly identifiable) value position' (2017, 19). The essence of their approach is sociological and comparative in form – the emphasis is on unpacking the social character of educational knowledge with attention to historical traditions embedded in national contexts, as the chapters by Schriewer (2017) and Paine (2017) effectively illustrate. An overview of the terrain of educational knowledge is developed through a degree of comparison and contrast, while acknowledging substantive differences in educational knowledge that persists internationally.

Furlong and Whitty (2017) do not seek to make conclusive judgements about the 'value' or appropriateness of the knowledge traditions they identify. This enables them to explore the character of various traditions of educational knowledge while not explicitly arbitrating between them. In some contrast, the later work of Bernstein (2000), and that of Wheelahan (2010) and Young and Muller (2016) takes a more distinctive position regarding forms of knowledge. Bernstein (2000) suggested that the values underpinning the disciplinary structures that had successfully produced specialised forms of knowledge since the enlightenment are under attack from a 'new concept of knowledge' that is 'divorced from persons' and 'their commitments' (86), and instead prizes knowledge for its instrumentality and its commercial value. Young and Muller (2016) have anchored their arguments on Durkheim and Bernstein, identifying how certain 'specialised' types of knowledge accrue the power to provide greater insight through the socio-epistemic conditions of their production and validation, including the manner by which knowledge is challenged and revised in communities of peers. The implication of these Bernsteinian and social realist approaches is that certain socio-epistemic conditions make it possible to make discerning judgements about claims to knowledge circulating in academic and professional communities. What is less immediately apparent from this work is the nature of the practice that underpins the specific socio-epistemic conditions by which knowledge can be challenged, progressed, revised and validated.

This approach to the evaluation of knowledge claims set out in Bernstein (2000) and Young and Muller's (2016) work requires a careful maintenance of disciplinary boundaries, implying a degree of autonomy and licensed discretion for the knowledge community and independence from direction from external parties (Bridges 2006; Hordern 2021). Whitty and Furlong's (2017) work indicates how aspects of such disciplined socio-epistemic dynamics operate in the context of educational knowledge in an international perspective. For example, the historical dynamics of disciplined educational thought in the German context appear purposeful and bounded (Schriewer 2017), clearly differentiating themselves from other disciplinary communities in higher education, and this contrasts with the more multi-disciplinary traditions that are characteristic of the Anglosphere (Furlong and Whitty 2017). The German version of hermeneutic educational thought revolves around key concepts and notions that are reflected upon and iterated continuously within the disciplinary tradition (Westbury, Hopmann and Riquarts 2000; Schriewer 2017), notwithstanding recent challenges from empiricism (Schriewer 2017).

On the other hand, Furlong and Whitty (2017) identify approaches to educational knowledge traditions that are less supportive of the development of distinctive disciplinary procedures for educational knowledge. Such knowledge traditions could be said to be rooted in a 'what works' logic that suggests that any claim to knowledge is ultimately to be tested against market imperatives or notions of relevance in the context of current policy agendas (Hordern, Muller and Deng 2021). If a claim to 'knowledge' has a direct practical use and secures results or outcomes that meet the approval of those in power or hold sway within a particular context, then it achieves validity. In such an instrumental vision, knowledge producers are not involved in a collaborative quest for truth but seek to establish their work as dominant within a market for the most (superficially) efficacious approaches. For some producers of educational knowledge, their reputation and livelihood may depend on it. This is antithetical to the Durkheimian or social realist approaches to establishing truth claims and achieving consensus on knowledge validity (Young and Muller 2016). An instrumental approach supplants disciplinary procedures for evaluating knowledge with measures and outcomes that are externally fashioned – the norms by which knowledge claims are evaluated are no longer internally generated and owned. The boundaries between the sacred/specialised and the profane/non-specialised are therefore irrelevant to a 'what works' knowledge tradition – the 'ongoing process in extended time' (Bernstein 1999, 161) that underpins disciplined knowledge production is impossible if knowledge is instrumentalised and there is no necessary reference to previous knowledge claims. All that matters, instead, is whether the knowledge input is perceived to contribute to whatever is desired as an outcome, which may be as simple as a change in a performance measure or adherence to a prevailing policy discourse.

Extending the sacred/profane differentiation to educational practice

Although academic institutions and the knowledge they produce have often been thought to characterise the 'sacred', and 'everyday' contextual work the 'profane', this can seem an impossibly restrictive distinction. Educational practitioners who have been educated in the 'sacred' world by studying at university or in teacher education institutions are exposed to ideas and concepts that they may carry with them as they practise in schools and other educational settings. However, these ideas may be perceived as irrelevant in the context of practice, or alternatively they may enable the practitioner to interpret practice differently, using a more refined lens. It is important to note here, as discussed in previous chapters, that what we think of as 'educational practice' can be construed very differently. Practice, if seen as representing the wide range of activities that practitioners are engaged in (a more attenuated approach, following Hager 2013), can comprise numerous notions, concepts and rules of thumb with potentially quite arbitrary criteria. Such an approach accords with Schon's (2001) characterisation of practice as a 'swampy low-land', but there are nevertheless different types of swamp, and various approaches to negotiating these. Moreover, the need for a negotiation through specific types of swampy lowland may give rise to various forms of knowledge that can assist in the negotiation of swamps more generally, and this can be gathered and distributed amongst practitioners. This 'theory-building' is often intended to be helpful to a wide range of practitioners, but comes at a cost if it becomes static and resists iteration, or does not engage with existing understandings. It is important therefore to unpack the relation between theory and what Furlong and Whitty (2017, 19) call the 'world of practice' in some more depth. As has been pointed out by a number of commentators (Guile 2010; Winch 2010) a simple dichotomy between theory and practice can be highly problematic, as it masks the nuanced relationship that exists between the two.

As has been established in earlier chapters when we consider the nature of practice we can start from two contrasting positions. We can either perceive practice as a basic category used to define all human (and perhaps non-human or human-material) activity, or we can see practice as inextricable from the knowledge and issues by and for which it is constituted. A considerable volume of practice theory suggests the former position suggesting that practice can be seen as, in Schatzki's (2010) words, 'an open organised array of doings and sayings' that are held together (perhaps temporarily) by 'rules' and 'under-standings'. In such a conception the human or human-material world can be seen as a 'seamless assemblage, nexus or confederation of practices' (Nicolini 2013, 3), and a useful research objective would be to identify the defining elements of, or phenomena associated with, any given practice, and how it relates to other practices. For Rouse, such a position could be described as a 'regulist' or 'regularist' conception of practice as they imply that habits and behaviours constitute practices when they are 'exhibiting a regularity' or are somehow 'governed by a rule' (Rouse 2007, 47). The observable regularity in itself is sufficient to constitute something called a 'practice'.

As detailed in the earlier chapter, what Rouse describes as 'normative' approaches to practice take a more refined view of the definition of practice. This position on practice requires that there is demonstrable 'mutual accountability' between the performances (or activities) of the practice, so that each action has a particular meaning and significance in the context of the practice. The meaning of the practice is brought about by the sense that something is 'at stake' (2007, 50) and thus there is value in engaging in the practice and performing it to a high standard. In turn, this implies that the practice will have some boundaries and develop some criteria which can meaningfully indicate what counts as constitutive of that practice, and what lies outside. In practices where processes of (specialised) knowledge generation, modification, circulation and exchange are central core activities, this normative version seems apposite, for example in the case of professionalised occupational practices, and in academic communities (Beck and Young 2005; Hager 2011; Hordern 2016). For those involved in generating specialised forms of knowledge in disciplinary communities something is clearly 'at stake', as that knowledge has a particular value to those who produce it and perhaps (in Young and Muller's 2016 conception) to society in general. A Durkheimian approach would suggest that such normative practices are necessary for the generation of 'collective representations' and common bonds between community members who recognise the character of specialised knowledge relevant to their society.

The notion of a specialised (or sacred) practice does require some nuance, however. Firstly, some professional or occupational groups (medicine) hold forms of social or moral authority that make it easier for them to 'control' the sacredness of their practice – and therefore to ensure that specialised knowledge is engaged with systematically in practice. Secondly, it is important to note that specialised concepts underpin a great deal of activity in modern life. Even in those contexts in which we are not consciously making use of specialised knowledge, forms of that knowledge may be necessary to make any given activity possible and are required for its successful execution (Hordern 2018; Young and Muller 2014). For example, the everyday use of computers in workplaces relies on the sophisticated technologies that drive such machines and the engineering that obtains the minerals that are used in component parts, and it is specialised knowledge underpinned by forms of specialised practice that enables this to happen. Specialised practices provide the socio-epistemic conditions by which scientific and engineering knowledge may be validated and iterated, and discarded and removed where no longer relevant to the practice purpose. When the conditions within a practice enable the examination of previous, existing and new ideas, theories and proposals with regard to their truthfulness and commitment to truth (Young and Muller 2007), and their appropriacy in the context of the normativity of the practice, then we can be more confident that 'good sense' is prevailing in the practice (Winch, Oancea and Orchard 2015, 209). This mirrors Durkheim's argument that concepts maintain validity through the 'indefinitely repeated test' that the 'men who adhere to it verify by their own experience' (2001, 333), although what is meant by 'experience' here has to be seen in the context of normative practice (and types of specialised acquaintance knowledge bound up with know that and know how as outlined above).

Any given practice may engage systematically in the examination of theory, generating new ideas with all practitioners participating in the ongoing development of knowledgeable forms of practice. However, practices can also be influenced by trends that lead the distortion of knowledge claims, or allow situations in which redundant theories survive unchallenged, or enable market or bureaucratic logics to dominate (Freidson 2001). No practice is likely to replicate the normative notions perfectly. We can thus differentiate educational practices by (i) the degree to which they are underpinned by specialised or non-specialised knowledge; and (ii) the degree to which the differentiation between those forms of specialised and non-specialised knowledge is recognised and acknowledged. This recognition and acknowledgement is evident if specialised forms of internally and externally negotiated disciplinary logic prevail over instrumental logics that suggest knowledge should be valued for its 'effectiveness' in supporting specific policies or commercial imperatives, which may be short-term in view. If practitioners are full participants in the practice and allowed to contribute to the development of shared conceptions of the practice purpose, then there is greater potential for knowledge value to be refined and mutually agreed within the practice, and procedures for establishing and recognising quality upheld. On the other hand, if practitioners are disempowered and not encouraged to engage in building shared conceptions of knowledgeable practice, and only receive instructions or dictates around the use of knowledge in practice then they may be less competent to make judgements about new techniques or innovations, and unable to contribute fully to the practice community.

The (re)shaping of different forms of professional practice and knowledge: some examples

It is possible that certain forms of practice are considered somehow distinctive or separate from trends that affect others. For example, some working within higher education may consider the context of academic practice as distinctly different from professional educational practice, but attempts to separate academic work may be misleading. As Beck and Young (2005) suggest, drawing on Bernstein (2000), the 'assault' from markets and governments pertains as much to academia and other professions as it does to occupations with less status in society. This assault entails a dismantling of professional control of knowledge via managerialism, resulting in a 'divorce' between 'knowledge' and the 'knower' (Bernstein 2000, 81), an eradication of the 'commitments' and 'personal dedications' (86) and the implicit assertion that 'accumulated knowledge' is increasingly superfluous and irrelevant to contemporary society (Beck and Young 2005, 191). Academic practice, particularly that which draws on accumulated knowledge, can be portrayed as a roadblock to the progress of the market. Specialised disciplinary knowledge can be portrayed as outdated or irrelevant, a barrier to the advancement of 'twenty-first-century skills' (as in, for example Robinson 2008), or to the rollout of educational reforms to curricula and teacher education that fit economic agendas.

If disciplinary knowledge (including that of art, design and drama as much as the sciences, history of languages) is replaced by an agenda focused on nebulous notions of skill, the loss is greater than just the content of the knowledge that enables practitioners to think beyond their experience, to hypothesise and to conceptualise. The destruction extends to professional identity, professional judgement and occupational commitment, which are all interdependent and reliant on a thriving form of professional knowledge (Bernstein 2000; Beck and Young 2005; Young and Muller 2014). By undermining specialised educational knowledge, governments or commercial enterprises are undermining the potential for committed knowledgeable educational practitioners capable of exercising reasoned judgements based on accumulated expertise. As Abbott's (1988) work on 'jurisdiction' and control over occupational activity suggests, in order to contribute to the development of educational knowledge, educational practitioners need some protection and preservation of their identity and autonomy to make judgements. While the boundaries between occupational jurisdictions may be permeable, if they are eradicated then the consequence is a loss of identity and expertise. However, jurisdiction can only be maintained in the longer term if occupational groups are able to demonstrate that they have a justifiable claim to authority over an area of expert work, and this can be shown through the efficacy of their practice in the pursuit of goods which have value to society (MacIntyre 2007), as the example of medical professionals illustrates (Abbott 1988; Foray and Hargreaves 2003).

The relationships between higher education, practitioners and the state enable the conditions for specialised knowledge and practice to emerge, and thus also the production of educational knowledge. Reflecting on accounts of the development of these relations over time in national educational contexts offers opportunities for conceptualising variants of these relations, and the potential implications. In Germany the role of educational professionals is underpinned by legislation enacted at state level, and 'higher education and the state worked together' to form 'licensure' that historically enabled teacher autonomy and *Didaktik* to flourish (Westbury, Hopmann and Riquarts 2000, 21). Educational professionals have therefore been provided with a high level of autonomy and control over their practice and enjoyed extended formation within higher education institutions, underpinned by powerful educational concepts which constitute an educational knowledge tradition (Westbury, Hopmann and Riquarts 2000; Schriewer 2017). These concepts and the thinkers behind them have served to constitute German educational practice as it is understood by educators there, providing it with a specialised character that can be distinguished from the 'everyday' or routine social interaction. In the German context the relationship between professional practice and higher education is intertwined, but this is underpinned by state licensure in a system that affords professional autonomy and discretion (Schriewer 2017). The conditions for specialised educational knowledge (produced and relayed by higher education), and specialised educational practice maintained by professional jurisdiction and underpinned by legislation, are held in place over time. But it would be erroneous to assume that this is immutable. The dominance of ideas of *Bildung, Didaktik* and the role of German educational thought in shaping educational practice has been criticised for inflexibility and inherent conservatism, and has been accused of being a major contributory factor in what has been seen as the poor performance of German students in international comparisons of student achievement (Ertl 2006; Schriewer 2017). Again, short-term external imperatives may serve to undermine the long-standing practice.

A contrasting example can be found in England, where reforms to teacher education over the last twenty years have increasingly foregrounded a governmental type of professionalism (Beck 2008), which have heralded new forms of prescription in the education and development of teachers, which has been accompanied by waves of government-led curriculum reform, inspection and systemic change (Whitty 2014). Higher education and disciplinary educational knowledge production have lost influence over the formation of educational professionals (Furlong 2013). Thus ideas developed in the foundation disciplines, which were identified as providing the academic base for educational thought since the 1960s in England have travelled less and less frequently or substantively into discussions and debates in educational practice contexts (Hordern, Muller and Deng 2021). Instead, those seeking to define appropriate educational practice increasingly look to the state, to the Department for Education teaching standards and to the latest reforms, rather than to any specialised educational knowledge traditions (Hordern and Brooks 2023). While many practitioners have been introduced to educational knowledge through previous courses, current forms of teacher preparation in England have very limited time for even a rudimentary introduction of disciplinary concepts and conceptualisations of education (Whiting et al. 2018). Instead a form of instrumental technicism holds sway (Winch, Oancea and Orchard 2015; Hordern and Brooks 2023), and as there is no compulsory licensure process controlled by the teaching profession that could unilaterally underpin a form of professional autonomy for teachers there is no effective counterbalance to government policy prescription.

As a consequence, governments in England have the means to play a more dominant role in shaping teaching practice in England than can be observed in Germany, and the relationship between higher education and practice has become fraught. Instead of higher education supporting and sustaining a specialised form of practice, the English experience is of a state which seeks to cast educational processes in service to a knowledge economy (Hordern, Muller and Deng 2021), and therefore aims to reshape practice into something that can meet these reform objectives without obstacle. While in Germany educational knowledge and practice have been accused of conservatism and inflexibility (Zierer and Seel 2012), the schools context in England is characterised by constant change and contestation over issues relating to the education of teachers, curriculum and pedagogic processes. The state and market-driven policy context in England sponsors 'what works' knowledge about education which has no reason to engage with previous disciplinary debates or 'accumulated knowledge' (Beck and Young 2005). This has occurred precisely because the macro-level objectives increasingly set by government for educational practice in England are themselves antithetical to disciplinary educational concepts (Hordern, Muller and Deng 2021).

Prior to the 1980s much teacher education in England was underpinned by the Foundation Disciplines of Education (Furlong 2013) (see also educational foundations in the U.S. and the discussion in Barrett and Hordern 2021). While these disciplines offer some substantive insights into educational practice, it is questionable whether the philosophy, sociology, psychology and history of education in the UK or in the US are based on a shared understanding of the 'educational phenomena' of concern to educational researchers, or of the problematics of educational practice. It could be argued that some studies of education policy or of the history of educational institutions, or of the role of education in social mobility, produce volumes of knowledge that concern education as a broadly understood phenomena, but are nevertheless not centrally concerned with core educational processes or concerns (i. e. issues of pedagogy, curriculum or assessment, or of holistic individual development in society). However, within the foundation disciplines there are also traditions of enquiry that maintain a clear focus on educational problematics. There is, for example, a significant body of philosophically and sociologically informed work conceptualising and problematising curriculum, and philosophically informed work conceptualising pedagogy and assessment (i.e. see Barrett and Rata 2015 and Barrett, Hoadley and Morgan 2017 for the use of one sociological tradition on curriculum). These foundation disciplines, partly because of their relationship to their 'parent disciplines' benefit from the capacity to self-regulate with a level of independence from external interests (although in the UK this is challenged by increasing performance management in higher education).

Turning specifically to reflect on the English context, while acknowledging parallels with the USA (Barrett and Hordern 2021), we can see that foundational disciplinary knowledge in higher education and the forms of educational knowledge it has produced have neglected to work with a more coherent vision of educational practice. While the foundation disciplines have presented a persuasive multi-disciplinary view of educational knowledge, the proximity and strength of the links maintained with other disciplinary traditions leads to a problematic relationship between educational knowledge and conceptualisations of practice. A key difference that we can observe that separates England from many continental European countries is the marginalisation of disciplinary traditions that focus on theorising educational conceptually in a manner that have resonance with the complexity and challenge of educational practice. This absence or vacuum in terms of educational concepts that could guide and bring together the educational research and practitioner community allows the notion of 'practice' in England to be captured and defined both by the government and by less than scrupulous 'edupreneurs' who are eager to advance their commercial positions through the sale of solutions to imagined educational problems. It seems reasonable to echo Brian Simon's (1981) point here that there remains no pedagogical tradition in England comparable to the continental European traditions in terms of conceptualising educational practice through distinctive educational thought. There would need to be a substantive change of direction in the relationship between educational research and practice to develop such a tradition. Without it, however, there are substantive limits on the extent to which educational practitioners are able to 'make good sense' (Winch, Oancea and Orchard 2015) of the practice they experience, or to resist the latest policies and interventions – many of which need either challenge or some serious questioning as to how appropriate they are for educational contexts.

In contrast to the foundation disciplines, there are traditions of educational knowledge outlined by Furlong and Whitty (2017) that are defined by their intention to produce knowledge relevant to educational practice, rather than answering to other disciplinary traditions. Some of these also explicitly rely on educational practice as a source and relay of that educational knowledge. As discussed below, these include clinical practice and networked professional knowledge (Furlong and Whitty 2017). While these are very distinct in their underpinning, approach and methodology, they are both characterised by a focus on the workings and potential of practice to generate knowledge, or to translate disciplinary knowledge for application in educational contexts.

In terms of clinical practice forms of specialised knowledge produced in the foundation disciplines are seen as an important element within a 'structured dialogue' that brings together 'diverse sources of knowledge' (including student data and teachers' conjectures about the learning context) with the aim of developing teachers' professional reasoning (Burn and Mutton 2015, 226). The method of clinical practice allows for specialised forms of knowledge to be considered alongside non-specialised local knowledge – and to stimulate forms of investigation and new insight into the practice context. However, there is also a risk that the character and potential of the specialised knowledge may be overlooked if its origins in the debates such knowledge emerges from are not recognised. If a clinical practice dialogue foregrounds specialised knowledge *only* for what it is perceived it can offer to help practitioners make sense of their specific practice contexts and to come to (potentially individualised) judgements about their approach to their practice, then the resonance of specialised knowledge *may* be lost. Some versions of clinical practice may slip towards an undifferentiated view of knowledge specialisation, if the reasoning process is shaped by a priority to produce teachers to meet current demands as they are shaped by current education policies, without considering alternatives or fostering the critical engagement that will enable alternatives to be considered. Without a coherent notion of educational practice as a specialised, knowledgeable activity, there is a risk that clinical practice can simply align with prevailing notions of practice pushed in government policy.

It is also possible that those involved in clinical practice select and transform specialised knowledge independently of those other propositional, inferential and procedural forms of knowledge that together provide that knowledge with its full meaning (Winch 2010; Hordern 2017). If this occurs, it becomes more difficult to see clinical practice as inherently specialised, although its focus on rigorous interrogation of knowledge and deepening professionalism (Burn and Mutton 2015, Furlong and Whitty 2017) indicate considerable potential for a more consistently specialised focus.

As a final example, the emergence of 'networked professional knowledge' (Furlong and Whitty 2017, 36–38) can be seen as a consequence of the levels of unhappiness and frustration with what are seen as the 'traditional hierarchies' (2017, 37) of foundational knowledge in education and the perceived lack of 'practical relevance' (37) of this knowledge. This has been fuelled by political environments in the Anglophone nations (the UK, USA) which have asserted that schools seek improvement through examining educational problems for themselves and developing their own versions of 'best practice' that can be distributed and refine through networks of practitioners. Arguably, this has become increasingly prevalent in both the USA and in England, making incursions within the spaces of educational thought previously reserved for different traditions and catching the eye of policy-makers and school leaders. Rather than acknowledging criteria for judging the truth and value of knowledge claims developed through disciplinary processes, networked professional knowledge concentrates on whatever is said to 'work in practice'. As a consequence, the idea of a community of practitioners charged with making judgements about revisions to knowledge seems irrelevant or redundant. There is no need to refer to previously existing educational knowledge. Instead, powerful agencies with influence over definitions of current practice, including inspection agencies, policy-makers and some school leaders (in terms of the English example), have much greater influence and are able to specify what counts as credible knowledge for educational practice. As Furlong and Whitty (2017, 36) note, this networked professional knowledge has much more in common with horizontal discourse than vertical discourse in terms of its focus on instrumental effectiveness. And with the lack of principle and avoidance of disciplinary process and structured participation the production of networked professional knowledge offers opportunities for magicians to market their educational fads to an audience that has been encouraged to ignore educational thought. While networked professional knowledge may appear to have answers to problems, such knowledge offers little in terms of the socio-epistemic processes required to sustain the type of professional knowledge required for the challenges of educational practice.

These last two examples of educational knowledge traditions are shaped to a much greater extent by non-academic educators than the academic field of the foundation disciplines. That said, there are some substantive differences in emphasis and orientation between them. On the one hand, we might see clinical practice as more clearly defined by its reliance on partnerships between higher education and research-inclined practitioners (Burn and Mutton 2015). The example of networked professional knowledge is perhaps most clearly separated from the epistemic arrangements of higher education, and offers new opportunities to those who situate themselves across the boundaries of the worlds of policy, educational practice and academia including influential figures in school improvement movements and politicians (Furlong and Whitty 2017). There is certainly a contrast between the speed with which networked professional knowledge can spread, and the connections that are made between this knowledge and policy and practice issues, and what might be perceived as more insular and slow-moving (although perhaps more rigorous and critically informed) approach of some academic work in education, with the foundation disciplines presenting one salient example.

What are the implications for how we think about specialised knowledge and practice?

The discussion above suggests that debates about educational knowledge and practice may benefit from a three-fold differentiation, which will shape some of the discussion in subsequent chapters. The first of these is to differentiate between specialised and non-specialised forms of educational knowledge (following Bernstein 1999, 2000, Durkheim 2001 and Young and Muller 2016), bearing in mind that the boundary between the 'specialised' and 'non-specialised' is ever-changing and iterating. A second differentiation needs to be made between specialised and non-specialised forms of educational practice, with a similar qualification as to the first differentiation around the inevitability of change. A third and perhaps frequently overlooked differentiation can be made between specialised *educational* knowledge and specialised *non-educational* knowledge. This third differentiation relates to the strength of the boundaries of education as a discipline or knowledge structure – the extent to which the nature of 'the educational' is clearly defined and forms a parameter for identifying what is considered *educational* knowledge production. In some research activities the boundaries are blurred and what is considered educational encompasses a wide range of studies that may have a bearing on education – education itself is defined in broad terms. On the other hand, it is also possible to envisage those involved in producing educational knowledge exercising greater 'restrictions over the phenomena they address' (Bernstein 1999, 164), potentially bringing a greater focus to disciplinary identity.

References

Abbott, A. (1988). *The System of Professions: An essay on the division of expert labour.* Chicago: University of Chicago Press.

Alderson, P. (2020). Powerful knowledge, myth or reality? Four necessary conditions if knowledge is to be associated with power and social justice. *London Review of Education*, 18 (1), 96–106.

Barrett, B. and Hordern, J. (2021). Rethinking the foundations: Towards powerful professional knowledge in teacher education in the USA and England. *Journal of Curriculum Studies*, 53 (2), 153–165.

Barrett, B. and E. Rata, (eds) (2014). *Knowledge and the Future of the Curriculum: International Studies in Social Realism.* London: Palgrave Macmillan.

Barrett, B., U. Hoadley and J. Morgan (eds) (2017). *Knowledge, Curriculum and Equity: Social realist perspectives.* Abingdon: Routledge.

Beck, J. (2008) Governmental professionalism: Re-professionalising or de-professionalising teachers in England? *British Journal of Educational Studies*, 56 (2), 119–143.

Beck, J. and M. Young (2005). The assault on the professions and the restructuring of academic and professional identities: A Bernsteinian analysis. *British Journal of Sociology of Education* 26 (2), 183–197.

Bernstein, B. (1999). Vertical and horizontal discourse: An essay. *British Journal of Sociology of Education*, 20 (2), 157–173.

Bernstein, B. (2000). *Pedagogy, Symbolic Control and Identity.* Revised edition. New York: Rowman & Littlefield.

Biesta, G. (2007). Why 'what works' won't work. Evidence-based practice and the democratic deficit of educational research. *Educational Theory* 57 (1): 1–22.

Bridges, D. (2006). The disciplines and discipline of educational research, *Journal of Philosophy of Education*, 40 (2), 259–272.

Burn, K. and T. Mutton. (2015). A review of 'research-informed clinical practice' in Initial Teacher Education. *Oxford Review of Education*, 41 (2), 217–233.

Department for Education (DfE). (2016). *Educational Excellence Everywhere.* London: DfE.

Durkheim, E. (2001). *The Elementary Forms of Religious Life.* Oxford: Oxford University Press.

Ertl, H. (2006). Educational standards and the changing discourse on education: The reception and consequences of the PISA study in Germany. *Oxford Review of Education*, 32 (5), 619–634.

Foray, D. and D. Hargreaves. (2003). The production of knowledge in different sectors. *London Review of Education*, 1 (1), 7–19.

Freidson, E. (2001). *Professionalism: The third logic.* Cambridge: Polity Press.

Furlong, J. (2013). *Education: An anatomy of the discipline. Rescuing the university project.* London: Routledge.

Furlong, J. and G. Whitty. (2017). Knowledge traditions in the study of education. In G. Whitty and J. Furlong (eds) *Knowledge and the Study of Education: An international exploration.* Didcot: Symposium, pp. 13–57.

Guile, D. (2010). *The Learning Challenge of the Knowledge Economy.* Rotterdam: Sense.

Hager, P. (2011). Refurbishing MacIntyre's account of practice. *Journal of Philosophy of Education* 45 (3), 545–561.

Hager, P. (2013). Practice as a key idea in understanding work-based learning. In P. Gibbs (ed.) *Learning, Work and Practice: New understandings.* Dordrecht: Springer, pp. 85–103.

Hammersley, M. (2005). Is the evidence-based practice movement doing more good than harm? Reflections on Iain Chalmers' case for research-based policy making and practice. *Evidence and Policy*, 1 (1), 85–100.

Hordern, J. (2014). How is vocational knowledge recontextualised? *Journal of Vocational Education and Training*, 66 (1), 22–38.

Hordern, J. (2016). Differentiating knowledge, differentiating (occupational) practice. *Journal of Vocational Education and Training*, 68 (4), 453–469.

Hordern, J. (2017). Bernstein's sociology of knowledge and education(al) studies. In G. Whitty and J. Furlong (eds) *Knowledge and the Study of Education: An international exploration*. Didcot: Symposium, pp. 191–210o

Hordern, J. (2018). *Recontextualisation and the education-work relation*. In S. Allais and Y. Shalem (eds) *Knowledge, Curriculum and Preparation for Work*. Rotterdam: Sense, pp. 68–88.

Hordern, J. (2021). Specialised, systematic and powerful *knowledge*. *London Review of Education*, 19(1), [6]. https://doi.org/10.14324/LRE.19.1.06

Hordern, J. and Brooks, C. (2023). The core content framework and the 'new science' of educational research. *Oxford Review of Education*, 1–19. https://doi.org/10.1080/03054985.2023.2182768.

Hordern, J., Muller, J. and Deng, Z. (2021). Towards powerful educational knowledge? Addressing the challenges facing educational foundations, curriculum theory and Didaktik. *Journal of Curriculum Studies*, 53(2), 143–152. https://doi.org/10.1080/00220272.2021.1891575.

James, M. (2012). Growing confidence in educational research: Threats and opportunities. *British Educational Research Journal*, 38 (2), 181–201.

MacIntyre, A. (2007). *After Virtue: A study in moral theory*. Notre Dame, IN: University of Notre Dame Press.

Muller, J. (2009). Forms of knowledge and curriculum coherence. *Journal of Education and Work*, 22 (3), 205–226.

Muller, J. (2014). Every picture tells a story: Epistemological access and knowledge. *Education as Change*, 18 (2), 255–269.

Nicolini, D. (2013). *Practice Theory, Work and Organisation: An introduction*. Oxford: Oxford University Press.

Paine, L. (2017). Framing education: Cautionary tales from the USA of the relationship between education studies and teacher education. In G. Whitty and J. Furlong (eds) *Knowledge and the Study of Education: An international exploration*. Didcot: Symposium, pp. 161–187.

Robinson, K. (2008). Changing education paradigms. Speech to Royal Society of Arts, London, 16 June.

Rouse, J. (2007). Social practices and normativity. *Philosophy of the Social Sciences*, 37 (1), 46–56.

Schatzki, T. (2010). *The Timespace of Human Activity: On performance, society and history as indeterminate teleological events*. Lanham, MD: Lexington.

Schon, D. (2001). The crisis of professional knowledge and the pursuit of an epistemology of practice. In J. Raven and J. Stephenson (eds) *Competence and the Learning Society*. New York:Peter Lang, pp. 185–207.

Schriewer, J. (2017). Between the philosophy of self-cultivation and empirical research: Educational studies in Germany. In G. Whitty and J. Furlong (eds) *Knowledge and the Study of Education: An international exploration*. Didcot: Symposium, pp. 75–99.

Simon, B. (1981). Why no pedagogy in England? In B. Simon and W. Taylor (eds) *Education in the Eighties: The central issues*. London: Batsford, pp. 124–145.

Westbury, S. Hopmann and K. Riquarts (eds) (2000). *Teaching as a Reflective Practice: The German Didaktik tradition*. Mahwah, NJ: Erlbaum.

Wheelahan, L. (2010). *Why Knowledge Matters in Curriculum: A social realist argument*. Abingdon: Routledge.

Whiting, C., Whitty, G., Menter, I., Black, P., Hordern, J., Parfitt, A., Reynolds, K. and Sorensen, N. (2018). Diversity and complexity: Becoming a teacher in England in 2015–16. *Review of Education*, 6(1), 69–96.

Whitty, G. (2014). Recent developments in teacher training and their consequences for the 'University Project' in education. *Oxford Review of Education*, 40 (4), 466–481.

Whitty, G. and Furlong, J. (eds) (2017). *Knowledge and the Study of Education: An international exploration*. Didcot: Symposium.

Winch, C. (2010). *Dimensions of Expertise: A conceptual exploration of vocational knowledge*. London: Continuum.

Winch, C., Oancea, A. and J. Orchard. (2015). The contribution of Educational Research to Teachers' professional learning – philosophical understandings. *Oxford Review of Education*, 41 (2), 202–216.

Young, M. and J. Muller. (2007). Truth and truthfulness in the sociology of educational knowledge. *Theory & Research in Education*, 5 (2), 173–201.

Young, M. and J. Muller (2014). Towards the sociology of professional knowledge. In M. Young and J. Muller (eds) *Knowledge, Expertise and the Professions*. Abingdon: Routledge, pp. 3–17.

Young, M. and J. Muller (2016). *Curriculum and the Specialisation of Knowledge*. Abingdon: Routledge.

Zierer, K. and Seel, N. M. (2012). General didactics and instructional design: Eyes like twins. A transatlantic dialogue about similarities and differences, about the past and the future of two sciences of learning and teaching. *SpringerPlus*, 1 (1), 1–22.

4

THE SOCIAL AND ORGANISATIONAL DYNAMIC OF PRACTICE

Introduction: How could and should practice be organised?

It could be reasonably argued that how practice is conceptualised has a considerable bearing on how we think practice could and should be organised and the social dynamic of that practice. A normative position might be seen to imply a consensual control of practice through a community of practitioners (i.e. MacIntyre 2007). Rouse's (2007) work can be seen as implying a consensual control of practice via a process of mutual accountability that eventuates through peer interaction according to established and agreed norms. This can arguably be seen as demonstrated within the processes of disciplinary communities (Bridges 2006), sharing ground with a distinctive professional logic (Freidson 2001) and in notions of knowledge-based professionalism outlined by Young and Muller (2014), and developed in some of my own previous work (Hordern 2014, 2016). A meaningful notion of 'practice' comes about through fora that offer practitioners opportunities to debate and agree on the standards by which practice activity can be normatively evaluated to iteratively produce internal and external goods. Thus practitioners themselves would need to have sufficient control in order to set and adapt norms, but the body of practitioners must comprise those who are committed to sustaining and iterating the criteria of excellence of the practice. We can therefore perceive a requirement not only for practitioners to be capable of critical reflection (based upon scholarship and research activity), but also for scholar-researchers to be in some sense practitioners – to be meaningfully and consensually part of a practice community focused purposefully on the practice itself, and cognisant of its objectives and relations with other practices.

DOI: 10.4324/9781003054474-5

In contrast, what Rouse calls a regulist or regularist conception of practice makes less of an implicit stipulation in terms of practitioner influence on the character of the practice. Practice activities can be seen as those which are obvious 'regularities' – they are those which currently habitually occur, and attention is thus turned to the activities that 'hang together' in a given architecture (Schatzki 2010) or those that are habituated and routine (Nicolini 2013). In such a context there is no necessity for normative questions to be raised in regularist understandings of practice (although this is not to say that such questions would not be raised). Rather, the emphasis in discussions of practices when thought of as exhibited regularities tends to be primarily on sophisticated description of activities with the use of various forms of qualitative research and forms of fieldwork, and a concentration on the development of complex theoretical models and frameworks that seek to interpret the relations between elements of the practice or simply to provide rich description (Hager 2013; Nicolini 2013). As a consequence, in these versions of practice many activities may become labelled as practices over which practitioners have no or limited control. Participation in the practice may be, in a sense, seen as unwitting or potentially involuntary. The practitioner may have become a participant in a regular habitual activity, such as a way of travelling to work or a routine of going shopping with friends which can be seen as part and parcel of their everyday existence, and not necessarily something they have subjected to deeper consideration. Within a regularist or regulist (or a 'more attenuated' (Hager 2013) conception) there is no need to consider the development of internal goods, or their relationship to external goods generated by the practice (to use MacIntyre's 2007 terms). There are no expectations of criteria being generated by which expressions of the practice can be evaluated, although these may potentially arise in some regularities over time. From the perspective of some practice theorists, it may well be that the idea of a normative practice would be seen as irrevocably connected with positions and perspectives that could be implicitly or explicitly imposing a set of dominant values on others.

In this chapter I explore these aspects of practice a little further by examining ways in which we might conceptualise its organisation and social dynamic, and the relation between the social and the epistemic within practice. To do so, ideas from various sociological and philosophical sources are considered in the context of the foregoing normative and less attenuated notions of practice. In particular there is a focus on the distinction between (i) church and magic in Durkheim's work; (ii) Bernstein's work on vertical and horizontal discourses; (iii) the generation of external and internal goods in MacIntyre's work and as discussed by Hager (2011); and (iv) the work of sociologists of knowledge such as Collins (1998) on interactional ritual chains in relation to intellectual communities and Eyal's (2019) discussion of the role of trust in the context of the development of expertise. All of these, it is argued, can contribute something to our understanding of the social and organisational dynamic of practice.

Durkheim's distinction between the social organisation of the secular church and magic

In his book on the elementary forms of religious life Durkheim (2001) develops a helpful distinction between the practices of an idealised version of the church and that of magic, which can serve to further illuminate the social dynamics of different practices, including their socio-epistemic underpinnings. Durkheim suggests that much of the visible character of the practices of this ideal church and those of magical societies are similar in the sense that both have central rituals that are explicit to both participants in the practice but also to those outside of it – magic has 'rites which are the mirror image of religious cere-monies', superficially resembling religious practice and expecting followers to demonstrate their adherence to these rites. But Durkheim argues that under-neath this superficial resemblance the relationship between the magician and his/her followers is ephemeral and hierarchical, as there are 'no lasting bonds' to maintain the practice community and magical societies 'never include the believers in magic only the magicians' (43–44). Magic can be effective in com-pelling those participating in its activities to a position of faith and adherence through rites and rituals – but once these are stripped away, little substance remains, and there is no opportunity for the believers to participate. They are followers of magicians rather than participants in the practice.

In contrast the idealised notion of the church that Durkheim portrays (at least as far as it can be understood as a template for a secular religion) can be seen as characterised by a nuanced type of inclusivity, with those participating 'bound to one another by their common beliefs' (42), with a 'common con-ception of the sacred world and its relation to the profane world' (42–43), incorporating 'worshippers as well as priests' (44) as 'members of a moral body' (43). It should be noted that the church–magic distinction does not necessarily suggest that any particular religious or secular community is more likely to resemble one or the other – indeed some communities that may seem to be church-like may instead demonstrate much more of the hierarchy and manipulation of the 'magic' template. It might also be argued that the more participatory and inclusive notions may appear utopian and unrealistic, with no specific community ever demonstrating a completely democratic structure where any worshipper can be a priest and vice versa. Nevertheless, the dis-tinction between the character of church and magic illustrates characteristics of differing practices, the communities that construct them and the extent to which participants can contribute to what counts as knowledge. The distinc-tion focuses our attention on issues of hierarchy and participation and how conceptions of knowledge may or may not become and continue to be shared across communities.

The distinction between organising practice along the lines of the partici-pative church model or the magical society approach is helpful for considering the structure of more normative knowledgeable practice. While some approaches to expert practice may deliberately collapse the distinction and rely on what seems to 'work' or deliver outcomes, offering magical solutions to meet the concerns of policy-makers, clients or politicians, other forms of practice value shared understanding and are supportive of the development of consensus, while seeking to maintain a clear distinction between knowledge that meets recognised standards of excellence and that which does not. In the idealised 'church' model, it is the community itself, and its historically developed precedents, which act as the ultimate arbitrators of knowledge value, while in the 'magic' model, the magicians are free to conjure up claims to knowledge without recourse to a community. In this magic model the primary objective is to keep 'followers' spellbound, captivated by the trick that the magicians have developed and eager for more. Such a phenomena has resonance in policy and practice in contemporary education, where we see demands for solutions to real and imagined problems from policy-makers and educational practitioners. These problems, which have often arisen as a consequence of previous policy and the interventions of previous magicians, become opportunities for new magicians to arise and sell their new tricks, with the aim of seducing a new stream of followers to their tradition.

Bernstein's vertical and horizontal discourses

Another useful framework to explore the social and organisational dimensions of knowledgeable practice is that of Bernstein's vertical and horizontal discourses. These distinctive discourses were developed to delineate between the specialised and non-specialised forms of discourse, including the knowledge, identity and consciousness associated with these (Bernstein 1999, 2000). On the one hand we are introduced to the vertical discourse (which is associated with a degree of symbolism, objectivity and 'distance' from its subject matter) and on the other to the horizontal discourse (associated with spontaneity, the 'subjective' and the undertaking of practical action) (Bernstein 1999, 158). Although much of the subsequent discussion around this element of Bernstein's oeuvre has focused on the implications of horizontal and vertical discourses for how we think about disciplinary and curricula knowledge, Bernstein was also aiming to show 'greater differentiation within and between these forms' and explore 'the social basis of this differentiation' (Bernstein 1999, 158). This differentiation has implications for how we think about forms of knowledgeable practice and the social organisation they entail.

In terms of horizontal discourse, which can be seen as 'set of strategies which are local, segmentally organised, context specific and dependent' (Bernstein 1999, 159) and can be seen as something as simple or banal as 'learning how to tie up one's shoes' or 'how to use the lavatory correctly' (160), the key is that the strategy (or practice) used is appropriate to the context. In horizontal discourse there is little in the way of 'systematic organising principles' with communication amongst those involved often based primarily on ' tacit recontextualising' (Bernstein 1999, 159) or perhaps on simple demonstration and imitation. What Bernstein describes as 'distributive rules' serve to 'structure and specialise social relations, practices and their contexts' and this –may relate to 'behaviour and expectations according to status/position' (159). Thus we can see how a child may learn to meet the expectations of their parents or their school in terms of dress or behaviour, or an apprentice may potentially learn a practical task through imitation and modelling (although we should not be lulled into thinking that primarily practical activities – such as expert crafts – are not specialised practice, as Gamble 2004 demonstrates from a Bernsteinian perspective).

Importantly, however, Bernstein leaves open the possibility that horizontal discourse can move beyond its 'segmented' nature and generate more general understandings through its processes of circulation and exchange. He asks, 'how is new knowledge freed from the local context and local agents of its enactment, and how does it begin to circulate?' (Bernstein 1999, 159). This leads him to consider the example of a 'fictitious community operating only with horizontal discourse', in which he makes the distinction between 'the set of strategies any one individual possesses and their analogic potential for contextual transfer', which he calls a 'repertoire', and the 'total sets of strategies possessed by all members of this community', which is termed a 'reservoir' (159). He suggests that 'the repertoire of each member of the community will have a common nucleus but there will be differences between the repertoires' (Bernstein 1999, 159). This 'common nucleus' arises through their membership of the same community and commitment to its continuation, and perhaps as a consequence of sharing some of the same experiences and problems. Horizontal discourse, after all, is concerned with the maximisation of 'encounters with persons and habitats' (Bernstein 1999, 159) with the aim of finding effective practical solutions to problems found in everyday life. While these 'strategies' may be 'local' and 'segmentally organised' (159) this does not mean they are not purposeful and willing to incorporate learning. It would be problematic therefore to dismiss the idea of horizontal discourse as not contributing at all to an idea of knowledgeable practice, even if it is unlikely to be helpful in conceptualising its primary processes. Indeed, if certain bonds, shared understandings, commitments and criteria are developed, such discourses may perhaps potentially acquire the characteristics of vertical discourses over time.

To explicate this further, Bernstein uses the example of 'a situation where one small-holder meets another and complains that what he/she had done every year with great success, this year failed completely. The other says that when this has happened, he/she finds that this "works". He/she then outlines the successful strategy' (1999, 160). Thus there are opportunities for learning and the generation of new knowledge, but the extent to which this will develop into a shared understanding is open to question without any broader social infrastructure which enables the communal consideration of these alternative strategies. If the 'common nucleus' is sufficiently strong, then this innovation – if it proves successful for both smallholders – may be brought to the wider community for their consideration and review. As Bernstein maintains: 'any restriction to circulation and exchange reduces effectiveness' leading to a privatisation of knowledge that limits the ongoing development of the smallholding practice and the greater development of the community that the smallholders are part of. If restrictions are applied, or the social infrastructure that enables the circulation and exchange is not maintained, then the processes of 'stratification' will lead to the production of 'distributive rules which control the flow of procedures from reservoir to repertoire' (1999, 160) and minimise the benefits.

Bernstein nevertheless emphasises that 'in the case of horizontal discourse, its "knowledges", competences and literacies are segmental. They are contextually specific and "context dependent", embedded in on-going practices' (Bernstein 1999, 161) and those practices may, we might conjecture, be ephemeral, albeit *potentially* part of a broader more normative practice. Bernstein suggests that horizontal discourse often comes 'with strong affective loading' and is 'directed towards specific, immediate goals, highly relevant to the acquirer in the context of his/her life' (161). While 'any one individual may build up an extensive repertoire of strategies which can be varied according to the contingencies of the context or segment' (161), it nevertheless seems unlikely to assume that any individual will always seek to act alone in gathering strategies, as most will see considerable benefits in working together with others in certain circumstances to resolve problems.

Bernstein also considers the processes by which knowledge is acquired in horizontal discourse, suggesting that the 'pedagogic interventions' are 'a function of the different "knowledges" required to be acquired', and emphasising that 'these "knowledges" are related not by integration of their meanings by some co-ordinating principle, but through the functional relations of segments or contexts to the everyday life' (Bernstein 1999, 160). As a consequence, 'what is acquired in one segment or context, and how it is acquired, may bear no relation to what is acquired or how it is acquired in another segment or context' (160). Each everyday activity (for example getting dressed for school and cleaning teeth) may bear little relation to the next in terms of a 'co-ordinating principle', but they are nevertheless 'segmentally related' (160) in that together they relate to an overall context.

In contrast to horizontal discourse, vertical discourse requires some form of co-ordinating principle that orientates its structure, and this is underpinned by a particular social dynamic that can be usefully compared with that of normative practice. As Bernstein says, the 'circulation' of ideas or claims to knowledge in vertical discourse 'is accomplished usually through explicit forms of recontextualising affecting distribution in terms of time, space and actors' (Bernstein 1999, 159), which might mean structured fora within which discussion can take place such as peer review processes and academic or professional publications. In essence 'circulation is accomplished through explicit recontextualisation and evaluation, motivated by strong distributive procedures' (Bernstein 1999, 159), that are reflective of the historical context in which the vertical discourse has arisen. While horizontal discourse appears quite ephemeral and subject to change if no longer considered immediately effective, there is a greater degree of stability and permanence implied in the notion of vertical discourse. This more specialised socio-epistemic structure resonates to a greater extent with the parameters and criteria of a normative practice, not least the sense that activities are accountable to each other, and also to a sense of purpose (Rouse 2007). It is important to note some caveats: Bernstein observes the critique that vertical discourse can result in a cutting-off, a 'disembedding of individuals from their local experiential world' (Bernstein 1999, 158), and notes the contrast Habermas makes between the 'instrumental rationality' (which might be associated with more vertical discourse) and the value of the 'life-world', which might be associated to a greater extent with the horizontal (158).

Bernstein argues that the 'integration of a vertical discourse is not integration at the level of the relation between segments/contexts as in horizontal discourse, but integration at the level of meanings' with vertical discourse consisting of 'specialised symbolic structures of explicit knowledge' (1999, 161), which arguably come with specialised identities and consciousness (Bernstein 2000). The procedures of vertical discourse are thus said to be 'linked, not by contexts, horizontally, but … hierarchically', while 'the institutional or official pedagogy of vertical discourse is not consumed at the point of its contextual delivery, but is an ongoing process in extended time' (Bernstein 1999, 161).

Discussing the social dynamic within which vertical discourse is acquired and circulated, Bernstein suggests that there are some considerable differences between the pedagogic acquisition of the vertical and the pedagogy of horizontal discourse. He states that 'the social units of the pedagogy of vertical discourse are constructed, evaluated and distributed to different groups and individuals, structured in time and space by "principles" of recontextualising' (1999, 161). These principles of recontextualisation are, arguably, embedded within the practice, although they may be subject to iteration in the face of new economic, political, social or technological demands on the discourse. The important point Bernstein raises is that principles for recontextualisation exist, but he neglects to discuss what might serve to generate and sustain such co-ordinating principles. It is here that notions of normative practice, in suggesting that continual deliberation and judgement relating to something considered 'at stake' for the practitioners (or of particular social value) (Rouse 2007; MacIntyre 2007) holds together practice over time, can be helpful for considering what is distinctive about vertical discourse. Where does a co-ordinating recontexutalisation principle emerge from without a normative practice to generate, adapt and restructure in accordance with what is considered 'at stake'?

Within vertical discourse, Bernstein delineates two archetypal structures, the horizontal and hierarchical, which relate to the social and physical sciences respectively. In the case of horizontal structures, which comprise a set of specialised languages (for example in the case of sociology, Marxism, functionalism, postmodernism), each 'new language offers the possibility of a fresh perspective, a new set of questions, a new set of connections, and an apparently new problematic, and most importantly, a new set of speakers' (Bernstein 1999, 163). When a new language emerges (for example a new social theory) it may well be 'taken up by the younger speakers of the particular horizontal knowledge structure' and 'used to challenge the hegemony and legitimacy of more senior speakers'. As a result, established theorists 'may be cut off from acquiring the new language because of trained incapacity arising out of previous language acquisition, and a reduced incentive, arising out of the loss of their own position' (Bernstein 1999, 163). Such a social dynamic suggests some disagreement and mutual incomprehensibility, which could load considerable tension onto the normative elements of the practice. Ultimately this could lead to the collapse of a vertical discourse, or perhaps more likely its consumption by other vertical discourses.

In the case of hierarchical knowledge structures such as the physical sciences the social dynamic is slightly different. In the case of these sciences 'opposition between theories in hierarchical knowledge structures is played out in attempts to refute positions where possible, or to incorporate them in more general propositions'. Very often 'at some point ... a choice is possible provided the issue can be settled by empirical procedures', suggesting that there is always an imperative to resolve disagreements empirically. This contrasts substantively with the 'case of a horizontal knowledge structure' within the social sciences, where 'neither of these possibilities are possible because the discreteness of the languages defy incorporations into a more general language' (Bernstein 1999, 163). Therefore the mode of engagement within the specialised practice of those producing and iterating the hierarchical and horizontal knowledge structures is likely to be distinctly different. Whereas the hierarchical structures may be influenced by a sense that previous understandings can be integrated within new findings – with new scientific discoveries potentially making previous theories redundant – those working with the horizontal structures such as the social sciences and humanities may be both more adherent to a particular lens or perspective (such as Marxism or functionalism in sociology) and potentially more content to allow a balance of differing perspectives to persist in their discipline (as I discussed in Hordern 2017). While these suggest slightly different modes of normative practice, the sense that there is something 'at stake' and that positions and understandings are 'always prospective' may well be strongly felt in both types.

It seems that both vertical discourse and horizontal discourse have something to offer to a consideration of the social dynamic and organisation of practice. Bernstein argues that 'both vertical and horizontal discourses are likely to operate with distributive rules that set up positions of defence and challenge' and that the 'structuring of the social relationships generates the forms of discourse but the discourse in turn is structuring a form of consciousness, its contextual mode of orientation and realisation, and motivates forms of social solidarity' (Bernstein 1999, 160). Whereas vertical discourse (with its hierarchical and horizontal knowledge structures) has the most overt alignment with notions of specialised and normative practice (including in terms of the social dynamic that MacIntyre suggests as discussed below), horizontal discourse is more fluid and contextual, with no necessity for a more normative practice to develop and reflect on shared understandings. This is not to say that horizontal discourse has no *potential* to develop the social dynamic of vertical discourse and to start to become more specialised and normative. The existence of the 'common nucleus' relating to a sense of social solidarity and the potential for the circulation and exchange of individual experience to lead to common understandings and further deliberation suggests a means by which the horizontal discourse can find a pathway to verticalise, if the society in which this discourse eventuates finds the matters with which it is concerned sufficiently important. Bernstein (1999, 2000) acknowledges that what any society holds as vertical discourse at any one time is subject the change. And any vertical discourse does not emerge out of a vacuum, but from the enquiries, circulations and exchange that are undertaken within some forms of horizontal discourse, which then over time become considered particularly valuable and requiring of a more complex social infrastructure.

MacIntyre's practice and Hager's commentary

MacIntyre provides the definition of practice as 'any coherent and complex form of socially established cooperative human activity through which goods internal to that form of activity are realised in the course of trying to achieve those standards of excellence which are appropriate to, and partly definitive of, that form of activity' (2007, 187). In so doing he raises the argument that practice can only be defined as such if it is somehow recognised as 'socially established' but also involves some form of co-operation amongst a group. For MacIntyre, similar to many other theorists of practice, there is an emphasis on a social dynamic that involves others in some form of collective enterprise. This definition also can be read as excluding those forms of activity that are somehow non-co-operative, which might include activities that participants are engaged in unwillingly. However, defining activities that people have no choice but to engage in leads to questions about free will, and also takes us to the points about social organisation and free participation raised by Durkheim in his contrast between the organisation of church and magic. MacIntyre's definition also excludes those activities which are not 'coherent and complex' which would encompass many of actions which we might see as simple, mundane or everyday (although these might potentially be components of a larger practice). And this coherence and complexity could also be extended to the types of social organisation needed to underpin such a practice.

The use of the term 'socially established' raises further questions about what 'established' might mean and how this might be interpreted differently by different groups. For some, a socially established activity might be only recognised as such as a consequence of the affirmation of powerful/influential groups in society. On the other hand, we might denote the extent to which an activity is considered established by the length of time it has been considered established, or the numbers of people involved in it, or some other form of societal recognition. The evoking of 'established' or establishment also can be read as inherently conservative – as something that has become established or socially embedded can be difficult to change, dislodge or terminate. Socially established activity can become dominated by those who led the establishing process and may remain central to the organisation of the activity and decisions about who can be admitted as a practitioner. This suggests a delicate balance to the notion of establishment and, arguably, a need for some fuller sense of how a practice can be changed over time by practitioners if required as a consequence of the environment in which that practice is set. For example, it might be argued that an educational practice needs to adjust to respond to a new institutional framework or a raising of a school leaving age – in such cases the organisation of the practice might need some reconfiguration so that the goods of the practice can continue to be generated for the students involved and wider society.

MacIntyre's discussion of the relation between internal and external goods is also relevant to the organisation of the practice and its social dynamic. As Hager (2011) identifies, MacIntyre has a tendency to make a clear distinction between internal and external goods. Hager summarises that for MacIntyre the internal goods of a practice are 'internal in two senses. Firstly, they can only be specified in terms of the particular practice, and, secondly, they can only be identified and recognised by the experience of participating in this practice' (Hager 2011, 547). These goods are thus to some extent definitive of the practice, and in the case of teaching have been foregrounded as distinctive aspects of educational practice (e.g. 'intellectual enthusiasm' and 'relations of care and trust'; Noddings 2003, 249). On the other hand, MacIntyre's external goods are benefits of the practice that could have been obtained in alternative ways and thus they are not exclusive to any particular practice (MacIntyre 2007). Hager identifies that MacIntyre's examples of external goods are 'prestige, status and money' and 'are always some individual's property and possession' (Hager 2011, 547). These external goods are thus seen in some way as in opposition to internal goods in MacIntyre's schema and as potentially problematic to the generation and sustenance of these goods. For example, in educational practice we might argue that a focus on undertaking educational activities primarily for the achievement of status or financial benefit would run counter to the internal relational and intellectual goods that Noddings (2003) discusses.

Hager (2011) seeks a reinterpretation of 'external goods' and argues that they should be sometimes seen as outcomes of a practice that are more widely beneficial. He discusses the example of the construction of a cathedral, arguing that 'buildings serve a social purpose, which is an external good to the practice of construction' (2011, 552). Thus, for Hager (2011) the boundary between internal and external goods is not always as clear cut as MacIntyre suggests, and there may well be external goods that have broader communal benefits well beyond the issues of prestige and status that may have contributed to bringing them into existence. Hager (2011) argues that external goods can often be 'morally neutral', even if 'morally dubious external goods (such as prestige, status and money) can and do come into play'. He suggests that we cannot automatically assume that the prominence of an external good in a practice serves to 'thereby render it morally suspect, even though a casual reading of MacIntyre might appear to suggest otherwise', and that 'in most practices it is important for their flourishing that there is a balance of internal and external goods' (Hager 2011, 553).

Hager's (2011) argument and example of social purposive external goods would suggest that the social and organisational dynamic of a normative practice could be considered a little more flexible than might otherwise have been the case. The kinds of activities that might be seen as central to a normative practice might contribute to whatever is considered 'at stake' through both the generation of internal and external goods (which might in themselves sometimes be indistinguishable), rather than seeing the internal goods as the only definitive elements of a practice. The idea of 'social purpose' through collective participation could result in outcomes of the practice that might be considered as external goods, even if the exercise of internal goods is inextricably bound up within their production.

On the other hand, another interpretation of MacIntyre's discussion of goods might suggest that the beneficial outcomes of practices are always to be seen primarily as related to internal goods and thus the distinction between the external and the internal should maintain. And such outcomes of internal goods could be seen as covering both physical assets (such as cathedrals in the case of construction for a religious and community purpose) and phenomena that educational practice would seek to generate (as in Noddings' work). In the end it may be that the phrase 'external goods' in using the term 'goods' has slightly confused the conversation. Such a reading would suggest that MacIntyre's view on the social organisation of practice may have a closer resemblance to that of Durkheim and Bernstein in tracing the production of beneficial 'worldly' outcomes back to an 'inner dedication' or a notion of a secular church that can only be maintained through certain forms of social organisation which deliberate on that which is 'at stake' and yet hold that as still only 'prospective' (Rouse 2007) and therefore open to change and iteration, while maintaining standards of excellence and criteria of judgement (Addis and Winch 2019). This interpretation would therefore turn us back to a sense that the social dynamic of normative practice is closer to that suggested by previously discussed authors – the 'symbolic order' offered by a normative practice requires a particular sociality that is distinctive and finely balanced (Young and Muller 2013; Eyal 2019; Hordern 2021). The outcomes of such arrangements matter, nevertheless, as demonstrations of what the practice offers to society – of its social value. The practice is thus somehow constitutive of society, and the society constitutive of the practice.

Further work in the sociology of knowledge: Collins and Eyal

To provide a broader look at work that might further deepen our understanding of the social character of practice it is useful to turn briefly to other sociologists of knowledge who are interested in expert practice and the circumstances in which ideas are husbanded and developed over time. Randall Collins (1998), in his book the *Sociology of Philosophies: A Global Theory of Intellectual Change*, provides a compelling and extremely comprehensive analysis of the socio-historical development of communities of ideas in a range of global contexts, including Greece, China, India and Western Europe. Collins is interested in how networks develop around ideas that persist over generations and produce some of the influential developments in knowledge that have shaped the character of the contemporary world. He presents a 'sociological theory ... which tells us the conditions under which symbols are generated and are felt to be morally and cognitively binding', which he calls the 'theory of interaction rituals' (Collins 1998, 20). He suggests that the focus on particular specialised and ritualised forms of interaction 'connects symbols to social membership, and hence both to emotions of solidarity and to the structure of social groups' (20). He focuses on the 'dynamics of networks' and the 'meshing of chains of local encounters' (21), arguing that the rituals undertaken 'ubiquitously in everyday life' are not dissimilar to the 'formal religious rituals which Durkheim analyzed' (21). Religious rituals can simply be seen as 'archetypes of interactions which bind members into a moral community, and which create symbols that act as lenses through which members view their world' (21–2), but these are not the only rituals to be found in 'complex societies', where 'every fleeting encounter' can be seen as a 'little social order, a shared reality constructed by solidarity rituals ... by the little marks of respect which idealise selves and occasions' (22).

Collins argues that an interaction ritual (IR) is composed of 'ingredients' such as the assembly of two or more people, who all 'focus attention on the same object or action ... aware that the other is maintaining this focus', while sharing a 'common mood or emotion' (1998, 22). Through the shared focus of attention and shared mood provide opportunities to become 'united in a shared reality' with participants feeling they are 'members of a group, with moral obligations to one another', with their 'relationship symbolised by what-ever they focused on during their ritual interaction' (22–23). For Collins, 'individuals who participate in IRs are filled with emotional energy, in propor-tion to the intensity of the interaction' likening this to Durkheim's 'moral force'. An IR 'charges up individuals like an electric battery, giving them a corresponding degree of enthusiasm toward ritually created symbolic goals when they are out of the presence of the group' (23), as these 'encounters have an emotional aftermath' that gives direction and purpose to the 'interior lives' and 'individual trajectories' of those involved (23). The IRs that form, and the networks that eventuate create 'long term contours of interactional chains' which are concomitant with the ideas that are a consequence of the interactions and the 'interior' pursuits of those who have benefited from them (Collins 1998, 53). The 'inner dedication' that Bernstein (2000) suggests is so impor-tant for the production of specialised knowledge is fostered by an emotional energy that is nevertheless not straightforwardly produced. As Collins under-lines: 'the flux of interactional ritual chains determines not merely who will be creative and when, but what their creations will be' (1998, 53).

Without delving further into the detail of Collins's very comprehensive study of the sociology of intellectual history it is clear to see the resonance of his work with the discussions of Durkheim, Bernstein and (to a considerable extent) the notions of normative practice outlined by Rouse and its expression in MacIn-tyre's work. Collins, like Bernstein, is substantively influenced by Durkheim's work on the relation between knowledge and society, and presents a model of intellectual practice that relates strongly to Durkheim's discussion of the idea-lised church and concerns about the more autocratic model of magical societies. Collins's interaction rituals can be seen as a contemporary expression of Dur-kheim's work, drawing on the micro-sociology of Goffman, and demonstrating how social solidarity is maintained through forms of social interaction. The social dynamic of Bernstein's vertical discourse, with a concern for making claims and debates explicit to those concerned with the knowledge structure, dovetails with Collins's insight into how specialised communities are sustained through suitably accessible interaction rituals that can spread emotional energy and maintain the focus and mood of the community (often at an international scale). The sense of the mutual accountability and appropriacy of actions that is highlighted in Rouse (2007) also resonates with Collins's focus on a shared understanding and mood, as do the notions of there being something 'at stake' (Rouse 2007) which provide the opportunity to 'focus attention on the same object or action' (Collins 1998, 22). Such intellectual communities use their interaction rituals to develop and maintain the sense of purpose through gen-erating emotional energy. Whether they are able to nurture a sense of 'pro-spectivity' (Rouse 2007) and refine their 'standards of excellence' (MacIntyre 2007) in the face of challenges thrown up by social, technological, economic and environmental change may be one factor influencing the extent to which they can maintain their chains of interactional rituals over a longer period.

It is useful also to briefly note the recent work of Gil Eyal (2019), who has highlighted the delicate balance of trust that is needed to sustain expertise in such specialised communities, and indeed in broader society. As part of his diagnosis of the origins of the crisis of expertise that he perceives in contemporary society, Eyal emphasises how trust is constantly at risk of fragmentation in a context in which many previous certainties have been challenged and exposed. The longstanding networks of expertise, held together perhaps by normative forms of practice and the interaction ritual chains that Collins (1998) discusses, are under pressure as a result of challenges to the 'reputation and credibility of scientific institutions, experts, expert systems and government agencies' (Eyal 2019, 62), which have been brought about through exposure of the numerous inadequacies, inconsistencies and failures of these in responding to contemporary problems. Trust is needed in these institutions and the expert practices that maintain them, but it is coming into question through the media, public participation and increasingly in the political sphere. Eyal identifies that a great deal of 'normal science depends on trust between scientists' and that 'they rely on informed trust, on reputation, and on collective assessments' (2019, 44) of the skills, competence and integrity of their fellow scientists in order to pursue their work.

This 'virtual witnessing' or 'internal trust' that is needed for scientific work to sustain does not, Eyal (2019, 44) argues, translate easily over into 'external trust'. While the communities of normal science which he evokes are seen as necessary for the functioning of a modern industrialised society, the support of the public is not guaranteed. While this internal trust may develop in communities that mirror the idealised church, and within those which generate vertical discourse or those that resemble the communities that pursue MacIntyrean practices, there is no guarantee that the outcomes of these practices receive the support and affirmation of the wider public. Internal trust may develop through the social solidarity offered within the interaction rituals, and the chains that support these, but there are always some who sit outside these ritual chains, practices or communities. These non-participants may or may not be members of other similar organised groups or communities, but whichever it is they are likely to need to be persuaded that the practice has some ongoing value and wider benefit to secure their support. As Eyal (2019) explores, the breakdown of trust with certain communities can have consequences for expertise, and result in new configurations of expert communities that may be better suited to meeting the challenges facing society (whether these are in terms of public health, education or the environment, to give some prominent examples).

Summary

In summary, this chapter has explored some substantive sociological and philosophical sources which can illuminate how knowledgeable, specialised or normative types of practice can be organised. The insights of Durkheim, Bernstein, MacIntyre, Rouse, Collins and Eyal each have something to offer to considerations of the social dynamic of knowledgeable practice, and the structure of the communities that can support such a practice. Establishing that issues of agreed purpose, participation, principle, interaction, and trust are key to the organisation of such communities, offers a way forward for thinking about how knowledgeable practice can arise and be sustained, but also how it can be undermined and fall apart.

References

Addis, M. and Winch, C. (2019). Introduction. In M. Addis and C. Winch (eds) *Education and Expertise*. Chichester: Wiley, pp. 1–20.

Bernstein, B. (1999). Vertical and horizontal discourse: An essay . *British Journal of Sociology of Education*, 20 (2), 157–173.

Bernstein, B. (2000). *Pedagogy, Symbolic Control and Identity* (2nd edn). New York: Rowman & Littlefield.

Collins, R. (1998). *The Sociology of Philosophies: A global theory of intellectual change*. Cambridge, MA: Belknap.

Durkheim, E. (2001). *The Elementary Forms of Religious Life*. Oxford: Oxford University Press.

Eyal, G. (2019). *The Crisis of Expertise*. Cambridge: Polity Press.

Furlong, J. (2013). *Education: An anatomy of the discipline. Rescuing the university project*. London: Routledge.

Furlong, J. and Whitty, G. (2017). Knowledge traditions in the study of education. In G. Whitty and J. Furlong (eds) *Knowledge and the Study of Education: An international exploration*. Didcot: Symposium, pp. 13–57.

Freidson, E. (2001). *Professionalism: The Third Logic*. Cambridge: Polity Press.

Gamble, J. (2004). Retrieving the general from the particular: The structure of craft knowledge. In J. Muller, B. Davies and A. Morais (eds) *Reading Bernstein, Researching Bernstein*. London: RoutledgeFalmer, pp. 189–203.

Hager, P. (2011). Refurbishing MacIntyre's account of practice. *Journal of Philosophy of Education*, 45 (3), 545–561.

Hager, P. (2013). Practice as a key idea in understanding work-based learning. In P. Gibbs (ed.) *Learning, Work and Practice: New understandings*. Dordrecht: Springer, pp. 85–103.

Hordern, J. (2014). The logic and implications of school-based teacher formation. *British Journal of Educational Studies*, 62 (3), 231–248.

Hordern, J. (2016). Knowledge, practice, and the shaping of early childhood professionalism. *European Early Childhood Education Research Journal*, 24 (4), 508–520.

Hordern, J. (2017). Bernstein's sociology of knowledge and education(al) studies. In G. Whitty and J. Furlong (eds) *Knowledge and the Study of Education: An international exploration*. Didcot: Symposium, pp. 191–210.

Hordern, J. (2018). Educational knowledge: Traditions of inquiry, specialisation and practice. *Pedagogy, Culture and Society*, 26 (4), 577–591.

Hordern, J. (2021). Why close to practice is not enough: Neglecting practice in educational research. *British Educational Research Journal*, 47 (6), 1451–1465.

Hordern, J., Muller, J. and Z. Deng (2021). Towards powerful educational knowledge? Addressing the challenges facing educational foundations, curriculum theory and Didaktik. *Journal of Curriculum Studies*, 53 (2), 143–152.

MacIntyre, A. (2007). *After Virtue: A study in moral theory* (3rd edn). Notre Dame, IN: University of Notre Dame Press.

Nicolini, D. (2013). *Practice theory, work and organisation: An introduction.* Oxford: Oxford University Press.

Noddings, N. (2003) Is teaching a practice? *Journal of Philosophy of Education*, 37 (2), 241–251.

Rouse, J. (2007) Social practices and normativity. *Philosophy of the Social Sciences*, 37 (1), 46–56.

Schatzki, T. (2010). *The Timespace of Human Activity: On performance, society and history as indeterminate teleological events.* Lanham, MD: Lexington.

Winch, C. (2010). *Dimensions of Expertise: A conceptual exploration of vocational knowledge.* London: Continuum.

Young, M. and Muller, J. (2013). On the powers of powerful knowledge. *Review of Education*, 1 (3), 229–250.

Young, M. and J. Muller. (2014). Towards the sociology of professional knowledge. In M. Young and J. Muller (eds) *Knowledge, Expertise and the Professions.* Abingdon: Routledge, pp. 3–17.

Young, M. and J. Muller (2016). *Curriculum and the Specialisation of Knowledge.* Abingdon: Routledge.

5

FROM EVIDENCE-INFORMED PRACTICE TO KNOWLEDGEABLE PRACTICE?

Introduction

As we have seen from the earlier chapters the notion of 'practice' as a phenomenon emerged from philosophical and sociological work. Hager (2013) has shown that theorists of practice draw on distinct philosophical and sociological traditions: prominent theorists are said to be indebted to Aristotle, Heidegger or Wittgenstein, or to employ a notion of practice within a broader social theory (i.e. Bourdieu or Giddens). Rouse has suggested that there are two principal schools of thought in the definition of practice: on the one hand those that are 'regularist' or 'regulist' (2007, 48), and on the other the 'normative' tradition. The regularist or regulist traditions portray practice as relating to habituated patterns of activity, or presuppositions (e.g. drawing on Bourdieu, but also certain strands of philosophical work – Heidegger and Wittgenstein), and therefore encompass a very wide range of human activity. In contrast, the normative tradition requires practices to have agreed purposes, communities, and criteria of excellence (MacIntyre 2007; Hager 2011, 2013) against which activity can be assessed (see also Winch 2010), and this tends to draw more on an Aristotelian foundation. Rouse (2007) highlights the 'complex relations of mutual interaction', a sense that there is something at 'issue and at stake' in the practice, and an agreement that any 'resolution' of issues is 'always prospective' (2007, 50–51) in normative practice. Thus there is an acknowledgement that the practice may be subject to continual change and adaptation as new revelations and understandings emerge. Arguably an openness to change is necessary to ensure the ongoing health and viability of the practice.

Building on the essence of MacIntyre's (2007) work, Hager (2011) outlined a version of practice that is useful for considering what might be distinctive about occupational and socially purposive practices, by identifying the

DOI: 10.4324/9781003054474-6

complex relationship between internal and external goods produced in practice. He suggests that the tangible external goods produced by purposive practices (i.e. a building resulting from the practices of construction or architecture) are in some sense outward realisations of the internal goods of the practice: the external and the internal are closely intertwined in such practices. From a different angle but also engaging with MacIntyre, Noddings has argued that teaching is a 'relational' practice generating internal goods 'directed primarily toward the growth of students' (2003, 250) and involving the generation of 'growing intellectual enthusiasm in both teacher and student, the challenge and satisfaction shared by both in engaging new material' and 'the awakening sense (for both) that teaching and life are never-ending moral quests' (2003, 249). By setting out such criteria and a sense of what is 'at stake', teachers' activities can therefore be evaluated normatively, providing a community of teachers (or educational practitioners) has a sufficiently clear understanding of the criteria by which the internal goods can be judged. It could reasonably be argued that normative traditions can help explain why certain activities sustain over time as viable purposeful practices that are underpinned by committed communities. The notion of a normative purposeful practice could also help address why some practices fall apart, unable to agree on a meaningful purpose to which they are directed and lacking in criteria or standards of excellence by which performance of the practice can be judged. The normative focus on consensually agreed purposes, the development of criteria of excellence and practitioner mutual accountability are therefore important areas of investigation for those interested in practices.

This chapter focuses on the notion of 'evidence-informed practice' in education and explores how this relates to the notions of normative practice and knowledgeable practice, as developed thus far in the book. It is asserted that in 'evidence-based' or 'evidence-informed' practice how both 'evidence' and 'practice' are conceptualised is often reductive and limited, overlooking the need for a normative conceptualisation of practice to develop criteria by which evidence can be judged against existing knowledge and understanding. The chapter provides an illustration by examining some recent discussion of evidence-informed practice in England both in academic and professionally orientated publications, and noting some similar developments in the United States, while also exploring some recent reform proposals in Australia that relate to the discussion. These do not generally support the development of systematic educational knowledge, knowledgeable practice, or deeper educational understanding amongst teachers and other educational practitioners.

As is also outlined elsewhere in this book (see Chapter 6), practice theories are used extensively in studies of professional and workplace learning (Gibbs 2013), and have influenced studies on teacher education and professional development. On the other hand, much literature on school improvement and on teacher learning is stuck with an immutable separation between 'theory' and 'practice'. Practice is seen as equating to just what educators do in their workplace settings (i.e. including teaching in schools, making judgements in the course of classroom interaction, etc.), while theory is often linked solely to knowledge produced external to the practice, by research organisations and academics (e.g. Muijs and Reynolds 2011, and see the critique outlined in my earlier article (Hordern 2021a)). Furthermore, an assumed separation between theory and practice is also manifest in academic work on the sociology of educational and professional knowledge (Young and Muller 2014 or Furlong and Whitty 2017). While the separation of the two may be useful analytically, the relationship between them is rarely subjected to more extensive consideration.

While a conceptual separation between theory and practice is often assumed in everyday professional life, and arguably is also useful for some forms of research and analysis, it can also be questioned. From the perspective of a normative conceptualisation of practice, it can be argued that the distinction is erroneous in that 'theory' (or a form of symbolic understanding) can only meaningfully be generated within a specialised form of practice which constitutes the criteria of excellence by which activity seeking to contribute to the practice could be evaluated. Any notion that theory can come before practice is therefore problematic, although there is no doubt that knowledge can be recontextualised between practices (often across generations – as discussed below). Nevertheless, the generation of criteria by which practice can be evaluated (as part of the process of 'theorisation') is important to ensure the practice is sustainable and durable and does not dissolve into disconnected individual activities. The criteria can only be constituted through the enactment of the practice, or by acquaintance with and engagement in practice activities – the 'theory' and 'practice' are thus inseparable, interwoven and mutually constituted. However, this still conjures further questions about how the practice adapts to new developments (either in terms of knowledge, but also economic or technological change) that may have bearing on the practice. All practices generate forms of knowing and being, some of which crystallise into explicitly articulated theories – much of that which could at some point be theory is therefore initially situated, tacit, or embedded within phronetic wisdom (Duguid 2005) and may remain so. The challenge is to avoid stasis, ensuring that whatever is explicit or tacit continually iterates to meet new problematics.

A more nuanced relationship between theory and practice does not, however, negate the potential for forms of specialised knowledge to sit outside specialised practices, at least temporarily. Historical work on the development and use of practical and technical knowledge provides a case in point. There are examples of classical engineering knowledge being selected and transformed over a thousand years later to address problematics posed by technological advance in the early modern period. Valleriani shows how 'sixteenth century hydraulic and pneumatic engineers appropriated ancient science and technology' (2014, 127), in this case Hero of Alexandria's text 'Pneumatics', with the aim of enhancing the practical efficacy of their technologies. This was undertaken through commentaries on Hero's original text, resulting not only in further technical knowledge but also in the 'elaboration of the theoretical principles of pneumatics' (172). The specialised knowledge generated in the ancient classical age was to an extent rediscovered and re-applied to new problems at a much later date. As I identified in (Hordern 2021b), the processes of systematisation, documentation and recording (and therefore making knowledge explicit) enable knowledge to sit independently of a practice, although it will take a specialised practice to be able to reactivate that knowledge and evaluate its use in relation to new problematics in new contexts. This has relevance for the discussion on 'evidence' and 'practice' – evidence produced by others (at a previous time and in a different context) could be pertinent for contemporary practice. However, the recognition of the value and purchase of that evidence for a particular practice requires the conditions of a normative practice to exist contemporaneously so that practitioners can make judgements about how that evidence may need to be adapted and transformed to make sense within the practice.

'Evidence-informed practice' and its prescriptions

It is interesting to consider to what extent these normative and knowledgeable notions of conceptualising knowledge and practice register against contemporary discussions of evidence-informed practice. This can be achieved through examining how evidence-informed practice (EIP) has been portrayed in recent educational reform in England. Notions of evidence-informed practice permeate much of the discussion about education policy in England (see DfE 2016, 2019), but also in the publications of many of the professional bodies concerned with education (Scutt 2017; BERA 2018). The increasingly central role of the Education Endowment Foundation (EEF) as the government's preferred arbiter of the 'best available educational research' (DfE 2019, 10), charged with 'independently' assessing and endorsing the 'underpinning evidence' (DfE 2019, 2) presented as a basis for initial teacher education in England, also raises questions about the marginalisation of knowledgeable practice in English education policy. In the section below the discussion begins with a focus on how EIP is seen by the Chartered College of Teaching, the still relatively new professional body for teaching in England, by summarising and further developing an analysis of how evidence-informed practice is presented in their first issue of *Impact* (see my discussion in Hordern 2019), the journal they started producing in 2017.

In May 2017 the Chartered College of Teaching published its first (interim) issue of *Impact*, a new journal. This issue had a specific focus on 'perspectives on evidence-informed education', foregrounding the problematic of better 'connecting research and practice' (Scutt 2017, 1). The choice of the first issue made sense if the overall objectives of the new journal itself are considered, with the purpose to have 'a tangible effect on classroom practice and, subsequently, on the outcomes of young people' (Scutt 2017,

1). The introduction previews articles that 'explore the question of what we mean by evidence-informed practice' and the issue incorporates a section in which teachers explain how they have 'implemented a concept from a piece of published education research in their practice' (Scutt 2017, 1). Throughout the issue there is a consistent separation maintained between 'theory' and 'practice', and there is very limited discussion of the character of practice itself. There is a sense throughout that there needs to be a 'double transformation' (Biesta 2007, 2) – both of educational research and educational practice, with the objective of improving schooling and the work of teachers. What is seen as important is 'summarising the best available evidence in practitioner-relevant forms' and the subsequent 'translation into effective practice' (Coe 2017, 7).

There is a prevailing assumption within the contributions to *Impact* that there is something akin to a moral imperative for 'high-quality research and relevant examples' to be more effectively utilised to transform educational practice, with an 'expectation' that better 'application can improve education' (Kime 2017, 5). This comes with the argument that those who are in possession of the 'best available evidence' are best suited to develop the 'tools' so that 'decision makers' can use 'goal theory' to transform practice. This top-down approach seeks a transformation that will only be complete with the 'normalisation of evidence-informed education' (Kime 2017, 5–6). The assumed hierarchy between evidence and the (presumably uninformed) activities of practitioners sits in contrast to the basis for more nuanced normative understandings of practice, which would suggest that excellence criteria need to be iterated normatively through the practice itself with a body of practitioners who are sufficient engaged with the issues 'at stake' (MacIntyre, 2007; Rouse 2007; Hager, 2011).

The relationship between evidence and practice outlined in that first (interim) issue of *Impact* echoes much published academic work on evidence-informed practice (e.g. Nelson and Campbell 2017), with a separation maintained between the processes by which evidence is produced and the (much neglected) notion of educational practice. The imperative towards the necessary transformation of practice is seen in systemic terms that dovetail with wider school or system improvement objectives. The arguments made are frequently supported with data that is used to claim that measurable attainment can be improved through certain approaches to school organisation, management and pedagogical strategy. The position is held that current educational practice is frequently at fault – on the basis of measurements about attainment in specific areas – and that 'high quality' research evidence can reform it. There is limited or no countenance of alternative longstanding purposes of education (i.e. those outlined by Spiel et al. 2017 or Biesta 2010).

As an example, Nelson and Campbell's overview of definitions of EIP focuses primarily on defining 'evidence', rather than 'practice' (2017, 128), as an introduction to an elaboration on the differences between 'evidence-based, research-based or evidence-informed' (128) approaches. Practice is seen as a phenomenon which evidence should have an 'impact' (131) on, while acknowledging that practice itself generates evidence (132). Consequently, the core concerns of academics and policy actors, as much as practitioners, should be the 'integration' of different forms of evidence, and their 'mobilisation' and measurability (132). This example has much in common with the neglect of a conceptualisation of practice in other work – such as the British Educational Research Association 'close-to practice' statement (BERA 2018) (see discussion in Hordern 2021a).

It could be perceived initially that a version of the normative version of practice has some similarity with notions of EIP as a clear purpose to practice seems important in terms of driving through improvements to attainment. However, EIP is not about a continual prospective revision of practice involving practitioners or a debate about what is 'at stake' or 'at issue' in the practice. Instead, the focus of EIP is usually derived externally from the practice, and thus practitioners are often excluded, losing their capacity for change and adaptation. The overriding objective on which evidence and practice is required to focus is 'enhancing learning', by improving 'a measure of attainment, derived from a robust assessment process' (Coe 2017, 7–9), but this is not something that could have been said to have emerged through a normative deliberative process. While other ancillary objectives such as examining the introduction of 'assertive discipline with the aim of improving students' behaviour' (9) are also noted, these are seen in the context of supporting the prime objectives of improving attainment. Any criteria by which changes might be evaluated are to be arrived at via specific approved methodologies such as 'from well-run RCTs' which provide 'strong evidence' (Collins 2017, 15). It is these much-heralded methodologies that can provide the basis for the 'outcome measures' from which evaluation of 'interventions' can be determined (Coe 2017, 7–8). The methodological criteria by which improvements can be judged are therefore developed from outside of the practice, and practitioners have no hand in iterating or challenging these.

The Education Endowment Foundation as evidence provider

The English policy context provides a further illustration of how the translation of evidence into practice is to be systematised. The Education Endowment Foundation is held up by policy-makers in England as the leading voice on educational research and its dissemination. School leaders have for some time been steered towards a 'teaching and learning toolkit' which provides summaries of evidence and 'practical tools' that are 'designed to improve practice and boost learning' (EEF 2016). The DfE 2015–2020 Strategy emphasised that it is the 'continued growth of the Education Endowment Foundation' that will provide the teaching profession with the 'high-quality evidence about "what works"' (DfE 2016, 17). This served to position the EEF as arbiter of the quality of educational research, a pattern that has been continued with the recent Core Content Framework for initial teacher education in England (Hordern and Brooks 2023). Underlying this is a belief that educational practice is about improving attainment in explicit, measurable ways, and about 'what works in raising the achievement of the poorest student' (EEF 2018, 1). This is also about asserting that educational practice is best improved by the provision of 'evidence presented crisply and cleanly, stripped of academic jargon, to inform their decision-making' and that there is a 'real appetite among teachers and senior leaders' for this evidence (EEF 2018, 2). And it is asserted that 'more than half of senior leaders are using it (the evidence provided by the EEF) to inform their own decision-making' (1). Any existing knowledgeable practice in education is seen as evidently redundant in the face of the supposedly superior evidence of the EEF (Hordern, Muller and Deng 2021).

The existence of the EEF also provides further insight into how norms may be produced for practice and the notion of 'mutual accountability' may be compromised in EIP. If bodies such as the EEF are given privileged status in distributing the 'best available' evidence with the aim of transforming practice, the consequence may well be an increasing stipulation of what is considered acceptable and expected in educational practice. The norms introduced by the EEF are not necessarily shared by other educational practitioners, many of whom may hold different views of the purposes of education or the range of ways in which students may achieve or progress. Any idea of mutual accountability is beside the point here as the overriding policy objectives of the education system hold sway, along with a technical view of teaching in which teachers are provided with recipes for how they are expected to improve their teaching to align with the evidence (as mandated according to a definition of quality set by the EEF and ultimately its chief sponsor, the DfE). There are also consequences stemming from the focus on EIP and the role of the EEF on how teaching professionalism is constructed, in that autonomy and discretion in educational practice is inevitably constrained, notwithstanding any advantages in teachers being 'evidence-informed' (Stoll 2017, 11). If teaching practice is restricted and constrained by an EEF-sponsored version of 'what works' in education, there are limited prospects for other practitioners (teachers and researchers) to have a stake in the practice and weigh the evidence themselves. More generally, it has recently been argued that the focus on evidence is a paradigm that has now become embedded in education policy (Helgetun and Menter 2022), and therefore the logic may transcend the existence of any one organisation or policy framework.

The role of the EEF as the UK government's preferred authoritative voice on 'evidence-informed' educational knowledge has echoes of the role of the Institute of Educational Sciences (IES) and the What Works Clearinghouse (WWC) in relation to the federal government in the United States. While the federal structure of the US adds considerable diversity in terms of the organisation of education systems and the preparation of teachers, the No Child Left Behind Act of 2001 and the Educational Sciences Reform Act of 2002, followed more recently by the Every Student Succeeds Act of 2016, provide a framework whereby the 'evidence-informed' claims of the IES and the WWC have come to have considerable influence in contemporary educational policy in the US, notwithstanding ongoing debate as to why the evidence fails to translate straightforwardly into practice 'improvements' (Farley-Ripple et al. 2018). As Paine points out, the foregrounding of the IES and WWC, in 'consolidating federal research dollars' and 'review panel criteria' around an evidence-led approach to educational research, leads to a situation in which 'other questions – what a phenomenon is in education, how it is experienced, what its meaning might be in a particular context or for particular actors ... gets crowded out' (2017, 166).

Many traditions of academic educational research are sidelined in such models of EIP and evidence management, as recent studies of government policy towards teacher education have demonstrated, including more deliberative traditions that are predicated on more normative and knowledgeable notions of educational practice (Hordern and Brooks 2023). However, this is not to suggest that all academic traditions would support a more normative practice perspective: some philosophies of practice, as discussed in Chapter 2, sit in contrast to some of the normative notions discussed above. Some sociological approaches to practice overwhelmingly focus on unpacking issues of power and elitism, relayed through language and informal networks and cliques. From the sociology of professions there is also the issue of how forms of autonomous professional organisation can sometimes lead to elitism and professional closure (Larrson 1977; Freidson 2001). While there is considerable value in this work, exposing power dynamics does not in itself invalidate arguments for a distinctive form of professional logic and practice, particularly if we see such professions and their practices as constitutive of society itself. It can reasonably be argued that educational practice is of such importance to society that teaching must be considered a professional practice requiring specialised knowledge and a degree of autonomy, developed with a sense of purpose that has resonance amongst practitioners (Winch 2010; Hordern 2015).

Evidence, educational expertise and the underpinnings of practice

It is important also to ask what can be meant by evidence in EIP, and to discuss how this relates to notions of educational knowledge and the professional expertise which teachers need to develop through processes of professional development (Hordern 2019). Winch (2010) argues that expertise is not only related to 'know-that' propositional knowledge, but also the capacity to make inferences between those propositions and the capacity to recognise and use the procedures for establishing the validity of claims to knowledge. This also needs to be supplemented, not least in professional practice, with deep acquaintance with the context of practice which the expert is participating in. This rounded and nuanced view of expertise also implies that practitioners with limited experience may well need periods of pedagogical guidance and support to master an appropriate understanding of the expert knowledge base. This also entails a subtle process of mastering how expert knowledge relates to individual cases and situations so that well-grounded judgements can be made. In this view the process of becoming an expert requires not only know-that, but also appropriate forms of know-how and experiences of the practice context. Furthermore, this view of expertise is also seen as intertwined with the capacity to exercise judgement with a degree of autonomy (Winch 2010), which again casts doubt on the systemic view of expertise embedded in EIP and the EEF. For Bernstein (2000) and Beck and Young (2005) expertise is also related to the development of a distinct identity which engenders commitment to the expert practice, and arguably this enables expert practitioners to perceive a practice context differently from others (Shalem 2014; Hordern 2016). A reasonable command of the requisite knowledge base and the development of a professional identity should also help experts to differentiate between activities which are not underpinned by appropriate expertise and those that are, at least in terms of the practice in which they participate.

Winch's (2010) model of expertise also suggests a specialised form of epistemic community has to be charged with the development of expertise amongst practitioners, and this community shapes the criteria which define the expert practice (Addis and Winch 2019). The community is responsible for establishing procedures by which knowledge claims are judged, and maintains the epistemic memory of the practice. Processes by which new developments are reviewed and evaluated also need sufficient expert practitioners with the commitment and understanding to undertake this review and evaluation (Beck and Young 2005). In terms of Rouse's (2007) discussion of 'mutual accountability', a set of established norms are generated which form the basis for judgements regarding new claims to contribute to the practice. Freshly developed 'evidence' or claims to knowledge are thus evaluated against existing propositions, and the conceptual web in which those propositions are located, to establish the significance of the claims made and their bearing on existing professional practice.

An examination of the work of the EEF in England or the Institute of Education Sciences (IES) in the USA suggests, however, that prevailing views of EIP do not acknowledge the salient role of a community for guaranteeing expertise, or consider the mutual accountability through which claims to knowledge (e.g. new evidence) should be reviewed and evaluated. The EEF does not incorporate a mutually accountable body of expert practitioners that represents the full range of educational knowledge (Furlong and Whitty 2017) and has not set up an expert community with appropriate academic review processes to evaluate its decisions and judge new claims to knowledge. In contrast, the EEF works with a specific view of what educational knowledge should focus on, and how educational practice should be transformed. Increasingly, the EEF is positioned to exert a hegemonic hold on definitions of what is acceptable in terms of 'evidence' about education in England through a promulgation of a 'gold standard' research approach (see Hordern, Muller and Deng 2021). Recent examples of how this plays out in practice have been documented in relation to the substance of the Core Content Framework for initial teacher education in England (Hordern and Brooks 2023), where the EEF alone has been positioned as the guarantor of the 'best available educational research' (DfE 2019).

According to the EEF, evidence is seen as specific new propositions, which can then be collated within the 'learning and teaching toolkit' to frame interventions in the education system. The evidence validated and authorised by the EEF (according to their preferred methodologies) is not available for challenge or continuous critique, as might be expected in an expert or disciplinary community. The idea is that evidence can be presented without academic jargon to bring about a step change in thinking about education in schools. A relatively narrow version of educational practice can be constructed and spread within the system partly through control of the 'evidence' which underpins best practice. However, this approach fails to acknowledge that this evidence-based system reform does not help teachers develop the capacity to make inferences between propositions and reflect on their work or help develop communities of expert educational practitioners with the capacity to assess new claims to knowledge. The evidence-based system underpinned by the EEF suggests that educational practitioners submit to an evidence authority, which is deliberately located outside of the main academic community (who some might think could subvert the overall policy). For the EEF and their governmental sponsors, the overall objective is to steer the ship of the education system towards the objective of raising measurable pupil attainment (in terms of tests and examinations) in English schools, and constructions of evidence and educational practice are expected to work towards that end.

The EEF or IES model of accumulating evidence leads to a situation in which evidence is 'selected', 'appropriated' and 'transformed' (i.e. recontextualised) (Bernstein, 2000) for the education system to meet an objective framed by policy. The objective of improving measurable attainment has not come about through deliberation within an expert community (which might bridge both academic and professional communities as it may do in health professions for example), but through a process of narrowing debate by marginalising other contributors. It entails a rejection of the educational academic community as represented in the UK by the foundation disciplines of education or in the USA by the educational foundations, which is to be superseded by applied educational research and what Furlong and Whitty (2017) call the 'new science of education'. The objective is determined by policy-makers – the improvement of measurable attainment as understood via indicators such as PISA and other global forms of measurement. Evidence is therefore selected and steered towards school communities via the learning and teaching toolkit according to a specific (and highly contested) understanding of the objective of education that has emerged outside the 'epistemic' or disciplinary educational community. The focus on a specific objective, and the evaluation of interventions on the basis (primarily) of this objective also entail a neglect of the potential 'side-effects' of the implementation of new interventions and strategies based on the evidence.

Furthermore, there is also the potential possibility that high-quality disciplinary research on education becomes evaluated only in terms for its utility in relation to prominent policy problems, as identified by government or school leaders. Again, following Bernstein (2000), disciplinary enquiry may be delocated from the domain in which it has been produced and then relocated into the 'evidence domain', where different parameters of value apply. There is a risk that once separated from its origins disciplinary work will be given consideration only when it can be used to support an intervention that is deemed appropriate. In Bernstein's (2000) terms the field of the production of educational knowledge is increasingly under pressure from the agents within the official recontextualising field. The consequence is that other forms of educational knowledge produced by disciplinary communities are increasingly excluded from discussions within the policy domain and the wider school system. The most recent product of this line of thinking, the Core Content Framework for initial teacher education in England provides an illustration of this takeover by the official recontextualising field, as it positions the EEF and the UK government as the key arbiters of what counts as 'evidence informed' educational knowledge (Hordern and Brooks 2023). This centralisation of state control over the knowledge that informs teacher education is not confined to England. In Australia there have been similar recent pledges to introduce a 'core content' for teacher education centrally through the Australian government. The 2023 report of the Teacher Education Expert Panel in Australia outlines plans to 'establish ... core content and mandate it in national accreditation', asserting that this content should reflect the 'knowledge and evidence-based practices' that underpin teaching (Australian Government 2023, 9).

Arguments have been made that the model of evidence selection now introduced for education in England and planned for Australia is putting education on the trajectory that medicine followed in the nineteenth and twentieth century towards a professional discipline underpinned by scientific thought, and throwing off the legacy of its pre-modern origins (Foray and Hargreaves 2003). The argument could be that education, if seen as still harbouring the remains of its origins as a 'pre-theoretical human practice' (Carr 2003, 254), is in need of a transformation so that it can acquire a suitably rigorous knowledge base that accumulates relevant evidence. An absence of a scientific knowledge base can be seen as problematic in terms of education policy as governments wish to provide justifications for their strategies for educational institutions, as part of their broader reforms to education. Education is cast as having a supply-side responsibility to develop the skills and attitudes required for the economy, within a global race to provide appealing economies for investment of globally mobile capital (Spiel et al. 2017). Without measurable evidence of progress (or lack of progress) policy-makers are unable to answer to those that question their strategies.

As Furlong and Whitty (2017) have shown, the study of education contains a range of different knowledge traditions which have different levels of embeddedness in each national context, and this can be seen as a somewhat diverse and confused picture – at least by outsiders. The diverse structure of educational research also provides material for those advocating for the perceived certainty provided by EIP and the work of the EEF. The comforting certainty offered by EIP may be welcomed by those working in schools and colleges – many of whom may be frustrated by the weak and confused picture of educational research. In England, and also when we consider the educational foundations in the USA (see Barrett and Hordern 2021), the foundation disciplines of the philosophy, sociology, history and psychology of education lack coherence due to their inclusion of a diverse range of sociological, philosophical, historical, anthropological, psychological and comparative disciplinary work (Whitty and Furlong 2017), and arguably also their differing problematics (Hordern 2017). Much of the knowledge produced within the foundation disciplines has been challenged by school improvement and effectiveness traditions that bridge the academic, policy-maker and teaching communities (Hordern 2017; Barrett and Hordern 2021). This scenario suggests that the study of education in England (and in similar ways in the USA and Australia) lacks the characteristics of a disciplinary community that systematically maintains a set of mutually accountable disciplinary norms (Whitty and Furlong 2017; Barrett and Hordern 2021). Thus the appeal of the certainty offered by the EEF and by EIP is fuelled further.

For those involved in producing educational research informed by the foundation disciplines there are at least two possible trajectories. Some knowledge production distances itself from the current concerns of policy and practice and seeks to protect itself within its own disciplinary space, perhaps by adhering ever closer to the communities of its 'parent disciplines' (such as philosophy, history or sociology). On the other hand, other researchers seek to move closer to the concerns of the policy domain and speak the language of the evidence era (Helgetun and Menter 2022), leading potentially to a taken-for-granted view of practice problematics as they are constructed by dominant voices (i.e. policy-makers, school leaders and the EEF). This may be fuelled by a demand to be heard by policy-makers (see discussion in Francis et al. 2017), but it could also be about ensuring maximum chances to secure funding and pursue academic careers – given pressures put on higher education institutions within the UK and global environment. The result can be that educational research becomes ever closer to the logic of the marketplace, a logic which arguably sits in opposition to that required to underpin the development of a collaborative professional educational community and to support the development of individual and collective expertise (Freidson 2001; Addis and Winch 2019).

However, it is easy to make the mistake of extrapolating what is happening in England, or Anglophone contexts more generally, to the global situation. In a number of continental European countries and in Asia there are distinctive conceptualisations of educational knowledge and practice that are predicated on more humanistic or social-democratic understandings of the relationship between education, society and the individual (Furlong and Whitty 2017, Deng 2020; Krogh et al. 2022), and these often provide more coherent and systematic alternatives to the narrower and more empiricist versions of EIP. As both Deng (2020) and Krogh et al. (2022) argue, these more humanistic and deliberative traditions can be exemplified in the notions of *Bildung, Erziehung* and *Didaktik* in German and wider European educational thought, where there is a focus on the unfolding of individual potential in relation to the contemporary challenges of society, and an emphasis on teaching as 'relational and hermeneutic' (Uljens and Ylimaki 2017, 3). As Deng (2023, 6) has more recently illustrated, such deliberative work is also strongly influential in Chinese pedagogical theory, for example in the work of Lan Ye on life-practice pedagogics, with its focus on 'purposeful social activities', 'individual formation' and the 'value of life and development of life awareness'. In such circumstances, the role of education is not so straightforwardly positioned as a facilitator of national economic performance, as we have seen recently in England, for example. However, it would also be mistaken to assume that such traditions are not challenged themselves (e.g. see Schriewer 2017 on Germany). The notions of educational practice understood by educational practitioners in teacher education (which often involves extensive university and professional study) or by experienced teachers in other countries sustains some future prospects for more normative versions of educational practice.

From EIP to knowledgeable practice?

The ascent of EIP can be interpreted as a contributory element of the drive by governments towards systemic 'improvement' in education systems and a concentration on teacher quality and performance as a means of achieving this. For many involved in educational policy and research, the current state of teaching practice lags behind the findings of the 'evidence-informed' and 'evidence-based' movement. For them this means that further efforts are needed to bring about the awareness of this evidence amongst those in practice, alongside a narrowing of what is considered to be high-quality educational knowledge. Nevertheless, attempts to bring practice in education up to speed with 'the evidence' is leading to a negation of wider educational purposes and an instrumentalisation of pedagogical relations. Unfortunately, the disparate nature of educational research does not easily allow for a robust challenge to these developments. While this phenomenon is perhaps particularly prevalent in the Anglosphere, the 'evidence-era' that Helgetun and

Menter (2022) identify has an impact internationally. As noted above, some continental European countries may sustain traditions of educational practice that can modify and counteract the focus on EIP, even though such traditions are constantly under pressure from more scientistic and empiricist arguments.

Can forms of knowledgeable practice provide a counterweight to the drive for EIP? The work of Cain (2015) provides examples of how engagement with research can shape practice, highlighting the value of 'space for long, focused discussions' involving not only the 'voice' of external research but also the voice of colleagues (2015, 491). This may be a localised route to developing better understanding and mutual accountability of decision-making, and the furthering of criteria by which claims to expertise can be reviewed and evaluated, and therefore move towards the essence of a knowledgeable practice. Nevertheless, such activities need to be underpinned by a substrate of knowledge production and criteria of excellence which involve a growing sense of disciplinary community. Most illustrations of specialised professional community (medicine, engineering, law, architecture as examples) are inextricable from forms of higher education, as there is a recognition that the socio-epistemic practices of higher education provide a strong guarantor of integrity, truthfulness and the most sophisticated articulations of excellence criteria (although these are always in need of ongoing review) (Young and Muller 2014). The voice that Cain (2015, 489) denotes as a facilitator of deliberative discussion on research may therefore be a key element (but not the only element) required for the development of a more bottom-up version of knowledgeable educational practice.

A potential lesson for knowledgeable practice, at least as this relates to schools and attempts at 'school improvement', might be for how we conceptualise school educational practice as distinct but nevertheless closely related to forms of higher education or disciplinary practice. We could see the mutual accountability of teachers as conceived not just in relation to other teachers within a school or subject community but also to the educational academic community, with implications for academic work in education. A more scholarly teaching profession needs a more thoroughly scholarly academic community, both with better understandings of the distinctive and specialised purposes of education. A more complete grasp and understanding of education means an educational lens that is distinctly different from the view that prioritises the market or issues of efficiency, and is grounded in a deeper acknowledgement of what education is hoping to achieve. A more knowledgeable practice also entails greater practitioner participation in defining what forms of evidence should be assembled and for what purpose: a more participatory and democratic determination and classification of evidence (and nuanced understanding of its role). Through such processes a more specialised professional practice can eventuate in which practitioners have greater agency and control and in which a more appropriate form of specialised knowledge for educational practice can emerge.

References

Addis, M. and Winch, C. (2019). Introduction. In M. Addis and C. Winch (eds) *Education and Expertise*. Chichester: Wiley, pp. 1–20.

Australian Government (2023) *Strong Beginnings: Report of the Teacher Education Expert Panel*. Canberra: Australian Government.

Barrett, B. and Hordern, J. (2021). Rethinking the foundations: Towards powerful professional knowledge in teacher education in the USA and England. *Journal of Curriculum Studies*, 53 (2), 153–165.

Beck, J. and Young, M. (2005). The assault on the professions and the restructuring of academic and professional identities: A Bernsteinian analysis. *British Journal of Sociology of Education* 26 (2), 183–197.

Bernstein, B. (2000). *Pedagogy, Symbolic Control and Identity* (revised edition). New York: Rowman & Littlefield.

Biesta, G. (2007). Why 'what works' won't work: Evidence-based practice and the democratic deficit of educational research. *Educational Theory*, 57 (1), 1–22.

Biesta, G.J.J. (2010). Good education in an age of measurement: On the need to reconnect with the question of purpose in education. *Educational Assessment, Evaluation and Accountability*, 21 (1), 33–46.

British Educational Research Association (BERA) (2018). *BERA Statement on Close-to-Practice Research*. London: BERA.

Brown, C., Schildkamp, K. and Hubers, M.D. (2017) Combining the best of two worlds: A conceptual proposal for evidence-informed school improvement, *Educational Research*, 59 (2), 154–172.

Cain, T. (2015) Teachers' engagement with research texts: Beyond instrumental, conceptual or strategic use, *Journal of Education for Teaching*, 41 (5), 478–492.

Carr, D. (2003). Rival conceptions of practice in education and teaching. *Journal of Philosophy of Education*, 37 (2), 253–268.

Coe, R. (2017). Evaluation: Why, what and how. *Impact: Journal of the Chartered College of Teaching*, interim issue, London: CCT, 7–10.

Collins, K. (2017). The importance of randomised controlled trials in education. *Impact: Journal of the Chartered College of Teaching*, interim issue, London: CCT, 14–15.

Deng, Z. (2020). *Knowledge, content, curriculum and didaktik: beyond social realism*. Abingdon: Routledge.

Deng, Z. (2023) Understanding life-practice pedagogics—a distinctively educational way of thinking and theorizing with Chinese characteristics. *ECNU Review of Education*. doi:10.1177/20965311231196313.

Department for Education (DfE). (2016). *DfE Strategy 2015–2010: World-class education and care*. London: DfE.

Department for Education (DfE) (2019). *ITT core content framework*. London: DfE. https://www.gov.uk/government/publications/initial-teacher-training-itt-core-content-framework.

Duguid, P. (2005) "The art of knowing": Social and tacit dimensions of knowledge and the limits of the community of practice. *The Information Society*, 21 (2), 109–118.

Education Endowment Foundation (EEF) (2016). Our mission. https://educatio nendowmentfoundation.org.uk/about/history/.

Education Endowment Foundation (EEF). (2018). Annual report 2017. https:// educationendowmentfoundation.org.uk/public/files/Annual_Reports/EEF_Annua l_Report_2018_-_print.pdf.

Farley-Ripple, E., May, H., Karpyn, A., Tilley, K. and McDonough, K. (2018). Rethinking connections between research and practice in education: A conceptual framework. *Educational Researcher*, 47 (4), 235–245.

Foray, D. and Hargreaves, D. (2003). The production of knowledge in different sectors. *London Review of Education*, 1 (1), 7–19.

Francis, B., Archer, L., Hodgen, J., Pepper, D., Taylor, B. and M.C. Travers (2017) Exploring the relative lack of impact of research on 'ability grouping' in England: A discourse analytic account, *Cambridge Journal of Education*, 47 (1), 1–17.

Freidson, E. (2001). *Professionalism: The third logic*. Cambridge: Polity Press.

Furlong, J. and Whitty, G. (2017). Knowledge traditions in the study of education. In G. Whitty and J. Furlong (eds) *Knowledge and the Study of Education: An international exploration*. Didcot: Symposium, pp. 13–57.

Gibbs, P. (ed.) (2013). *Learning, Work and Practice: New understandings*. Dordrecht: Springer.

Hager, P. (2011). Refurbishing MacIntyre's account of practice. *Journal of Philosophy of Education*, 45 (3), 545–561.

Hager, P. (2013). Practice as a key idea in understanding work-based learning. In P. Gibbs (ed.) *Learning, Work and Practice: New understandings*. Dordrecht: Springer, pp. 85–103.

Helgetun, J.B. and Menter, I. (2022) From an age of measurement to an evidence era? Policy-making in teacher education in England, *Journal of Education Policy*, 37 (1), 88–105.

Hopmann, S. (2007). Restrained teaching: The common core of Didaktik. *European Educational Research Journal*, 6 (1), 109–124.

Hordern, J. (2015). Teaching, teacher formation, and specialised professional practice. *European Journal of Teacher Education*, 38 (4), 431–444.

Hordern, J. (2016). Differentiating knowledge, differentiating (occupational) practice. *Journal of Vocational Education and Training*, 68 (4), 453–469.

Hordern, J. (2017). Bernstein's sociology of knowledge and education(al) studies. In G. Whitty and J. Furlong (eds) *Knowledge and the Study of Education: An international exploration*. Didcot: Symposium, pp. 191–210.

Hordern, J. (2018). Educational knowledge: Traditions of inquiry, specialisation and practice. *Pedagogy, Culture and Society*, 26 (4), 577–591.

Hordern, J. (2019). Knowledge, evidence, and the configuration of educational practice. *Education Sciences*, 9 (2), 70.

Hordern, J. (2021a). Why close to practice is not enough: Neglecting practice in educational research, *British Educational Research Journal*, 47 (6), 1451–1465.

Hordern, J. (2021b). Specialised, systematic and powerful knowledge. *London Review of Education*, 19 (1), 1–11.

Hordern, J. and Brooks, C. (2023). The core content framework and the 'new science' of educational research. *Oxford Review of Education*, 1–19. https://doi.org/10.1080/03054985.2023.2182768.

Hordern, J., Muller, J. and Deng, Z. (2021). Towards powerful educational knowledge? Addressing the challenges facing educational foundations, curriculum theory and Didaktik. *Journal of Curriculum Studies*, 53 (2), 143–152.

Kime, S. (2017). From intentions to implementation: Establishing a culture of evidence-informed education. *Impact: Journal of the Chartered College of Teaching*, interim issue, London: CCT, 5–6.

Krogh, E., Qvortrup, A. and Ting, S. (2022). The question of normativity: Examining educational theories to advance deliberation on challenges of introducing societal problems into education. In E. Krogh, A. Qvotrup and S. Ting (eds) *Bildung, Knowledge and Global Challenges in Education*. Abingdon: Routledge, pp. 171–202.

Larrson, M.S. (1977). *The Rise of Professionalism: A sociological analysis*. Berkeley, CA: University of California Press.

MacIntyre, A. (2007). *After Virtue: A study in moral theory*. Notre Dame, IN: University of Notre Dame Press.

Muijs, D. and Reynolds, D. (2011). *Effective Teaching: Evidence and practice*. 3rd edn. London: Sage.

Muller, J. (2009). Forms of knowledge and curriculum coherence, *Journal of Education and Work* 22 (3), 205–226.

Muller, J. (2014). Every picture tells a story: Epistemological access and knowledge, *Education as Change*, 18 (2), 255–269.

Nelson, J. and Campbell, C. (2017) Evidence-informed practice in education: Meanings and applications, *Educational Research*, 59 (2), 127–135.

Noddings, N. (2003). Is teaching a practice? *Journal of Philosophy of Education*, 37 (2), 241–251.

Paine, L. (2017). Framing education: Cautionary tales from the USA of the relationship between education studies and teacher education. In G. Whitty and J. Furlong (eds) *Knowledge and the Study of Education: An international exploration*. Didcot: Symposium, pp. 161–187.

Rouse, J. (2007). Social practices and normativity. *Philosophy of the Social Sciences*, 37 (1), 46–56.

Schriewer, J. (2017). Between the philosophy of self-cultivation and empirical research: Educational studies in Germany. In G. Whitty and J. Furlong (eds) *Knowledge and the Study of Education: An international exploration*. Didcot: Symposium, p. 75–99.

Scutt, C. (2017). Editorial: Connecting research and practice. *Impact: Journal of the Chartered College of Teaching*, interim issue. London: CCT, 1.

Shalem, Y. (2014). What binds professional judgement: The case of teaching. In M. Young and J. Muller (eds) *Knowledge, Expertise and the Professions*. Abingdon: Routledge, pp. 93–105.

Spiel, C. et al. (2017). *The contribution of education to social progress*. In Rethinking Society for the 21st Century. Paris: International Panel on Social Progress.

Stoll, L. (2017). Five challenges in moving towards evidence-informed practice. *Impact: Journal of the Chartered College of Teaching*, interim issue. London: CCT, 11–13.

Uljens, M. and Ylimaki, R.M. (2017). *Bridging Educational Leadership, Curriculum Theory and Didaktik*. Cham: Springer.

Valleriani, M. (2014). Ancient pneumatics transformed during the early modern period. *Nuncius*, 29(1), 127–173.

Whitty, G. and Furlong, J. (eds) (2017). *Knowledge and the Study of Education: An international exploration*. Didcot: Symposium.

Winch, C. (2010). *Dimensions of Expertise*. London: Continuum.

Young, M. and Muller, J. (2007). Truth and truthfulness in the sociology of educational knowledge, *Theory & Research in Education*, 5 (2), 173–201.

Young, M. and Muller, J. (2014). Towards the sociology of professional knowledge. In M. Young and J. Muller (eds) *Knowledge, Expertise and the Professions*. Abingdon: Routledge, pp. 3–17.

PART II

6

KNOWLEDGEABLE PROFESSIONAL AND VOCATIONAL PRACTICE

Introduction

It has been persuasively argued that a focus on differentiating the structures and purposes of types of knowledge is important for understanding the nature of professional and vocational expertise (Winch 2010, 2013; Young and Muller 2014). Winch (2010) demarcates between know-that propositional knowledge, various forms of know-how (including the procedural and inferential forms which are closely related to the acquisition and use of propositional knowledge) and knowledge by acquaintance. These forms are brought together with project management capabilities, transversal abilities and various forms of technical skill to constitute types of occupational expertise which are nevertheless occupationally specific (Winch 2013). Young and Muller (2014), in their book on expertise and the professions, draw on Bernstein's work on vertical and horizontal discourses, and Winch's (2010) work, to delineate between specialised and non-specialised forms of knowledge. Their thesis has substantial implications for professional and vocational education, in (i) foregrounding the importance of conceptualising specialised disciplined forms of knowledge for occupational practice and (ii) exposing the vacuity of non-disciplinary competence-based 'generic modes' (Bernstein 2000, 53), which prioritise 'trainability' (53), and an 'empty openness to future requirements' (Young and Muller 2016, 166). This perspective challenges the assumptions behind much vocational and professional education in the Anglosphere, where elements of non-specialised genericism are pervasive in narrow competency-based forms, as pointed out by Wheelahan (2007) and Allais (2012). If it is posited that demands for forms of specialised conceptual disciplined knowledge and expertise are central requirements for a large swathe of occupations as Clark and Winch (2004), Winch (2010) and Young and Muller (2014)

DOI: 10.4324/9781003054474-8

suggest, then this calls into question influential approaches that emphasise situated, relational and contextual knowledge, approaches that hold significant influence in a wide range of professional and vocational education (see some of the chapters in Billett et al. 2014).

In this chapter an argument is made for an extension of the differentiation of occupationally related knowledge into considerations of professional and vocational practice. Rather than foregrounding the contextual or situated nature of practice as a central plank for the understanding of occupational knowledge and activity, a position that underpins the work of prominent theorists such as Schatzki (2010) or Nicolini (2013), it is argued that the notion of differentiation can be extended to consider how forms of practice can be differentiated by their underpinning knowledge, and by the socio-epistemic and institutional conditions that shape how knowledge is recontextualised in practice (Bernstein 1999, 2000; Hager 2011; Hordern 2014a; Young and Muller 2014). This leads into an illustrative differentiation between specialised and non-specialised elements of occupationally relevant knowledge and the practices associated with these. While this argument concedes that knowledge forms in practice are often intertwined and sometimes almost inextricable from each other (Young and Muller 2014), it is suggested that greater awareness of differentiation within the categories of knowledge and practice can assist disciplinary and occupational communities in identifying what forms of knowledge and practice are most appropriate in education for an occupation. The foregrounding of knowledge specialisation in the conceptualisation of professional and vocational practice encourages a reconsideration of educational processes in the formation of practitioners, particularly in cases where situated knowledge has been afforded a central role at the expense of systematic knowledge.

The terms professional and vocational are used interchangeably in this chapter, as the argument is intended to have relevance to a wide range of occupations often considered professional or vocational in nature, indeed all those occupations in which practitioners rely to some extent on forms of specialised knowledge for their practice.

The rationale for differentiating forms of knowledge

According to Young and Muller (2013, 236–238) knowledge should be seen as 'material', 'real', 'emergent' and 'fallible', building on a realist epistemology and ontology (Moore 2007; Young and Muller 2007). This realism recognises that knowledge is marked with the social character of its production, but also that the social conditions in which knowledge is produced and recontextualised into curriculum forms are varied, with some forms of 'sociality' better equipped to exercise judgement on claims to truth (Moore 2007; Young 2007). The consequence of this argument is that certain forms of knowledge have particular power in offering the intellectual resources to conceive of alternatives to current scenarios, and to hypothesise and conjecture reasonably on potential futures. This is illustrated in Bernstein's (1999) vertical and horizontal discourses, where vertical discourse is 'coherent, explicit and systematically principled' (159) and therefore 'specialised' (Young and Muller 2014), and horizontal discourse or everyday knowledge which is 'local', 'context-dependent', 'tacit' and 'specific' (Bernstein 1999, 159), and therefore unsystematic and non-specialised. Vertical discourses are then further demarcated between 'hierarchical' and 'horizontal' knowledge structures, with the physical sciences held as archetypes of the former and sociology and 'cultural studies' of the latter (162–163). Bernstein's differentiation is supported with the assertion that many thinkers (see list in Bernstein 1999, 170) have employed similar forms of dichotomy to understand the social basis of human knowledge. Drawing on Bernstein, it has been argued that without differentiation between types of knowledge structure it is impossible to distinguish what should be prioritised in school, vocational and professional curricula (Young 2008; Wheelahan 2010; Young and Muller 2014).

The importance of differentiation between knowledge types is underlined if one considers the different origins and purposes of types of knowledge, and the relations between these. Some propositional knowledge or 'know-that' clearly has greater significance when considered together with related 'know-that' propositional knowledge (Winch 2010). Such propositions sit in relation to each other within broader conceptual architectures that form disciplinary knowledge structures 'joined up' through a 'chain of inferential relations' (Young and Muller 2016, 170–171). Becoming adept in disciplinary thought is only possible with the acquisition of the requisite forms of 'know-how' that relate to that discipline (Winch 2010; Muller 2014). As Winch (2010) explains, knowing the propositions must be concomitant with knowing how to make inferences between them – individual facts or ideas are rendered meaningless if we do not understand what can be inferred from them. Equally, knowing how to apply the relevant procedures to judge claims to knowledge is vital to ensure that the conceptual architecture remains intact and that new knowledge is absorbed to a discipline only when it further enhances existing understandings of the subject matter (Winch 2013). Forms of know-that and know-how that are constituent parts of these disciplinary architectures can be differentiated from those which are not part of such architectures. This is not to say that non-disciplinary/non-specialised propositional knowledge cannot be complex and related to other forms of non-disciplinary knowledge. Barnett (2006. 146) provides the example of the local, specific and yet complex knowledge held by taxi drivers relating to the towns and cities in which they work. A key difference, however, is that such architectures tend to assemble knowledge for particular, specific purposes that cannot easily illuminate other contexts – in contrast to specialised conceptual architectures that provide a form of general understanding and insight within the frame of that specialised practice that can be applied to support multiple contextual applications (Muller 2009; Winch 2010).

Some forms of knowledge are 'specialised to develop conceptually' (Young and Muller 2014, 8) as part of the construction of bodies of conceptual thought that can shed light on a range of contexts. Other forms of knowledge can be said to be 'specialised to a contextual purpose' (8), including those that relate to occupational practices where the pursuit of 'more elegant or efficient' (9) solutions to technical problems becomes a key driver of knowledge production. Young and Muller (2014) explain how these two forms of knowledge are intertwined in an 'irreversible twist' (9), influencing each other's progress. The specialised knowledge of conceptual generalities is often fuelled by the need to explain the science behind technical solutions, while the specialised knowledge of contextual purposes has frequently absorbed general conceptual understanding to short-cut a route to more promising solutions to problems (Young and Muller 2014). Occupations have experienced differing trajectories of knowledge production partly as a consequence of how the professional and disciplinary communities that relate to them are organised (Foray and Hargreaves 2003), but also because of contestations around the core purpose of the occupation. What we think of as specialised knowledge today has been strongly influenced by industrialisation and economic transitions, but although 'the boundary between different knowledge forms may have been breached' (Young and Muller 2016, 158), it is forms of conceptuality that fundamentally underpin specialisation and enable knowledge progress (Bernstein 2000; Young and Muller 2016). Providing access to the conceptual resources and ways of thinking inherent to specialised knowledge enables practitioners to think through the problems encountered in their occupational practice, to consider alternatives and to reject inappropriate solutions (Wheelahan 2010; Winch 2010; Young and Muller 2014).

However, differentiation between specialised and non-specialised knowledge in the realm of professional and vocational knowledge is problematic for two main reasons. Firstly, the formation and continuing professional development of practitioners involves both time spent in educational institutions and in workplace practice. This complicates differentiation by exposing novice practitioners, whether they are apprentices or students in higher education, to a wide range of curricula, pedagogic and workplace representations of specialised and non-specialised knowledge which they must somehow make sense of as part of the process of becoming a competent practitioner. Secondly, and relatedly, the knowledge base that best supports the development of practitioners must balance the requirements and imperatives of disciplinary knowledge assembled in educational institutions and knowledge produced in workplace practice contexts (Barnett 2006). This means that for most occupations a specialised knowledge base must be generated, iterated and made available to practitioners in ways that differ from processes within the 'purer' disciplinary structures of knowledge production, where the relationship between research knowledge and curriculum structure is relatively straightforward, at least in higher education. The curriculum of a Maths and History degree is traceable to how knowledge is organised and produced in universities and through research (Muller 2009), whereas the curriculum of an engineering or management degree must assemble its knowledge base from a wider range of sources, and take account of a wider range of 'stakeholder' demands, while also recognising how technological and practice-based developments are affecting the occupation. It is this more complex process of 'reclassificatory recontextualisation' (Barnett 2006) that can result in difficulties in developing curriculum coherence (Muller 2009) as a wide swathe of specialised and non-specialised knowledge forms compete for inclusion, drawing weight from multiple reference points. Errors of recontextualisation can emerge as the grounds for selecting appropriating and transforming forms of knowledge are more opaque than they are for purer disciplinary structures as I outlined in Hordern (2014a, 2014b). This complexity and potential confusion, both in the exposure of future practitioners and in curricula form, highlights the importance of differentiation.

Thus it seems important to consider the purpose of each element of professional and vocational knowledge, and how these elements relate to forms of practice. However, this raises the question of what is meant by professional and vocational practices, and how these practices may or may not be affected by their relation to forms of specialised and non-specialised professional and vocational knowledge.

The rationale for differentiating forms of practice

Many prominent contemporary theories of practice seem disinterested in any knowledge-based principle that might be used to differentiate between practices. Talk of practice 'architectures', 'doings', 'sayings' and 'relatings' (Schatzki 2010; Kemmis et al. 2014) posits practice theory as concerned with the study of constantly shifting activity that endlessly varies 'historically and geographically' (Schatzki 2010, 51). Practices are therefore seen as inviolably situated, temporally and spatially specific, and 'composed in the site where they happen' (Kemmis et al. 2014, 33). Notwithstanding some debate around how practices are constrained or shaped by 'dimensions of human sociality' (Kemmis et al. 2014, 30), or indeed by materiality (Rouse 2001), practice theory generally emphasises the amorphous or polymorphous nature of practice – each act may be variably shaped by contextual factors, and certain activities may 'hang together' (Kemmis et al. 2014, 31) by virtue of sharing some 'skills and understandings' (Schatzki 2001, 12). For Schatzki and many others (Schatzki et al. 2001) it is notions of 'shared embodied know how' (12), 'shared practical understandings' and 'tacit knowledges and presuppositions' (11) underpinning 'arrays of activity' (11) that constitute practices. Nicolini argues that 'a practice approach radically transforms our view of knowledge' and that knowledge is 'always a way of knowing shared with others' (2013, 5), implying that forms of knowledge are entirely dependent on the form of practice that constitutes them, and should be understood solely by reference to the social dynamics of the practice.

It can be argued that these theoretical considerations neglect (i) the differentiated nature of knowledge used within practice (Winch 2010; Young and Muller 2014), and (ii) how systematic knowledge may relate to practical forms of know-how and acquaintance knowledge and transform the knowledge we think of as 'tacit' and 'situated' (Winch 2010; Winch et al. 2015). The essence of many contemporary approaches to practice is to deny a principle of differentiation, arguing instead for a seamless web of overlapping activities with very permeable boundaries, or a 'total nexus of interconnected human practices' (Schatzki 2001, 11), in theorisations that are keen to resist the technical, bounded and the intellectual (e.g. Nicolini 2013).

Some forms of practice theory tend also not to deliberate on the purpose of practices, or rather on the fact that some practices are clearly more socially 'purposive' (Hager 2011) than others. Caught up in the pursuit of a definition of practice it is easy to lose sight of any means of delineating between the purposes of professional and vocational practices and whether different categories of practice might require distinctive forms of conceptualisation. The idea that forms of practice such as amateur dramatics can be conceptualised within the same analytic framework as social work, teaching or engineering work seems questionable. While drama for recreation clearly has a purpose and requires forms of skill for competent execution, its purpose is not occupational and its outcomes do not matter substantively beyond those engaged in its practice, in the ways that engineering, teaching or social work practice do. If we differentiate in terms of practice purpose professional and vocational practices assume a category that can be set apart from recreational or personal everyday activity. Such practices require particular forms of knowledge, accountability and community, and many are enacted to fulfil a societal purpose (Abbott 1988; Freidson 2001; Winch 2010; Young and Muller 2014). The factors or 'dimensions of human sociality' that shape professional and vocational practices are organised through jurisdictional struggle between different occupations for control over work (Abbott 1988), by the interplay between professional, market or bureaucratic logics (Freidson 2001), and by the requirements for co-ordination with others and for commitment to standards of competence and expertise. And these factors play out differently within different occupations, suggesting that within the category of 'professional and vocational practices' there can be further differentiation along the lines of varied requirements for forms of expertise, organisation and inter-professional co-ordination.

While much of what has become mainstream practice theory draws on philosophical arguments that 'highlight non-propositional knowledge' (Schatzki 2001, 10), MacIntyre's (2007) influential conceptualisation of practice offers scope for theorising a differentiation between practices that takes account of the differentiated nature of knowledge and the conditions through which it is recontextualised in occupational communities. MacIntyre's conception of practice is 'normative' rather than 'regulist' or 'regularist'

(Rouse 2007, 47), by which Rouse means that the practice is 'maintained by interactions among its constitutive performances that express their mutual accountability' (2007, 48). Norms thus mutually generated within the practice become the means by which the exercise of that practice can be evaluated (Rouse 2007; Winch 2010,), and practitioners held accountable for their membership of the practice community. As Rouse suggests, 'holding to account is itself integral to the practice' (2007, 48). Yet, the exercising of the 'holding to account' and the process of evaluation according to norms require forms of organisation, community and judgement which do not cohere easily with fluid, seamless and unbounded conceptualisations of practice knowledge and activity.

For judgements to be fair and equitable and to maintain 'mutuality' in occupational communities there must be a degree of explicitness and systematisation (Winch 2010) – a community built purely on situated embodied knowledge and judgement quickly falls apart as its criteria or rules for entry are only held tacitly and cannot be understood except through a lifetime of personal contact. Moreover, the promotion of situated contextual 'know-how' and embodied knowledge as a key element of occupational practice disregards the need not only for accountability to other community members but also to other occupational communities and to wider society, who expect a succinct expression of the role and expertise of the occupation and what can be expected from its practitioners (Abbott 1988; Freidson 2001). While situated and embodied knowledge undeniably have important roles within practical activity, to elevate these to the core underpinning of all practices ignores the role of the systemisation of knowledge over the last thousand years in all complex purposive practices (Muller 2009) – a process that is likely only to accelerate (Clark and Winch 2004; Young and Muller 2014). Furthermore, the foregrounding of the situated and embodied also ignores the extent to which these forms are reconfigured by engagement with systematic knowledge (Winch 2010; Winch et al. 2015).

Differentiation between types of professional and vocational practice

Professional and vocational practices can be differentiated from each other by *the character* and *the extent* of specialised knowledge underpinning that practice. And the character and extent of specialised knowledge in use within the practice is inextricable from the *socio-epistemic and institutional conditions* existent within the professional or occupational community. These conditions shape how judgements are made in practice and influence the extent to which specialised knowledge is made accessible to practitioners. While practices can no doubt be differentiated by other means, it is asserted here that differentiation on the basis of the type of the knowledge underpinning practice should be foregrounded in order to understand specialisation and expertise in practices, and to understand what forms of professional or vocational education may be most appropriate. It is the type of knowledge that underpins the practice that affords the profession or occupation its degree of specialisation and jurisdiction (Abbott 1988; Young and Muller 2014), and (ideally) supports the maintenance of 'internal goods' and 'standards of excellence' (Macintyre 2007).

The character of specialised knowledge underpinning a professional or vocational practice

As noted earlier, Young and Muller (2014, 8) identify two forms of specialised knowledge, that which is specialised to 'conceptual generality' and that which is specialised to a 'contextual purpose'. The general (conceptual development) form is found across many academic disciplines, while the more applied (contextual purpose) form is located to a greater extent in professionally and vocationally orientated disciplines or fields. However, the contextual purpose form of knowledge is also used systematically and within practice contexts to inform practitioner judgement and to help find solutions to new problems encountered in practice (Young and Muller 2014).

The relationship between the 'general' and the 'contextual purpose' forms of specialised knowledge is thus a means of differentiating between practices. Certain practices require high levels of specialised knowledge to meet the purposes of the professional or vocation. For example, professions such as medicine and engineering rely on 'general' specialised knowledge from the physical sciences, both as the knowledge base for those entering the professions and as the source of concepts that can fuel new forms of knowledge specialised to a 'contextual purpose' (Young and Muller 2014, 8) relevant to problems encountered by professional practitioners. The dynamic interaction between the two forms of specialised knowledge fuels knowledge production for the occupation and shapes demands on practitioners. As Hanrahan (2014, 117) notes, with reference to the International Engineering Alliance graduate attributes, engineers require an 'understanding of the natural sciences applicable to the discipline', 'conceptually based mathematics', 'engineering fundamentals' and 'engineering specialist knowledge', with conceptual innovation primarily occurring in how 'advances in the natural sciences ... feed into specialist applications' (118). A prospective medical or engineering practitioner must possess sufficient facility with 'general' specialised knowledge in order to progress to increasing facility with the 'contextual purpose' specialised knowledge, and thus to be able to undertake expert action and make expert judgements in practice. Participation directly in such a practice is therefore not sufficient in itself to acquire this specialised expertise, and even novice participation relies on a high level of familiarity with 'general' forms of specialised knowledge, as a route into acquiring familiarity with the particular 'blend' of knowledge pertinent to that practice.

In some professions or other occupations the relationship between the two forms of specialised knowledge may be relatively distant, with innovation primarily within the 'contextual purpose' form. For example, for professionals working in technical aspects of surveying the knowledge fundamentals underpinning the practice remain important over time but there is ongoing rapid innovation in applications and working practices, including through inter-professional collaboration (Cook and Chatterjee 2015). Still other professional occupations, such as social work and teaching, have a more fluid and contested relationship between the 'general' and 'contextual purpose' forms of knowledge (Muller 2009), with criticisms of the irrelevance of some of the psychological and sociological theories that have been 'applied' to shape the knowledge base of these occupations (i.e. see debates about teacher education in the UK as outlined in Furlong 2013). Partly this is because the 'general' pure disciplinary knowledge forms from which they are drawing (i.e. sociology and psychology) possess an array of 'specialised languages' (Bernstein 1999) which cannot be easily 'delocated' and 'relocated' independently of the disciplinary debates from which they have emerged (Hordern 2014b). An important broader point, however, is that the relationship between the two forms of specialised knowledge is not static – the trajectory of professional and vocational practices is historically contingent (Foray and Hargreaves 2003) thus suggesting the important role of broader institutional conditions in shaping the relationship.

Even in occupations where the latest advances in research do not have direct or immediate impacts on practice, familiarity with concepts derived from the relation between 'general' and 'purposeful' forms of specialised knowledge can be crucial for professional judgement – a construction engineer may draw on recontextualised mathematical and scientific knowledge to solve a novel problem which does not correspond easily to the cases he has knowledge of or has experienced (Hordern 2014a). Equally a teacher ideally relies on a bedrock of research-based educational theory to make reasoned judgements in practice (Winch et al. 2015) – an arrangement put at risk in England by current policy developments that neglect longstanding educational theory (Hordern and Brooks 2023). Thus recontextualised specialised knowledge provides the substrate both for many diagnostic frameworks which practitioners employ explicitly or implicitly to make judgements in practice (Abbott 1988), and is also employed to manage anomalous cases which require judgement and action outside of established routine diagnosis and inference. The practice of making such judgements is a specialised activity, in that familiarity with the purpose and use of specialised forms of knowledge is necessary to make sense of the occupational context.

The extent of specialised knowledge used in the professional or vocational practice

Practices vary considerably in the extent to which specialised knowledge is used. Some routinised practices may require very limited engagement with specialised knowledge. Production or warehouse operatives working to processes prescribed by their employers have little reason to consider specialised forms of knowledge in the workplace, although forms of specialised knowledge may underpin the processes which they enact. In other practices, it is non-specialised situated and contextual knowledge, in terms of forms of personal know-how, market knowledge and social networking that enables practitioners to maintain an advantage in a competitive marketplace. This can be seen in occupations such as recruitment consultancy (Muzio et al. 2011), and in some of Muller's (2009, 218) 'particular occupations' such as travel agents or those working in hospitality or sales, who rely primarily on forms of interpersonal competence or knowledge of current market information to succeed at work. Additionally, there are many semi or unskilled occupations which involve practices that have limited discretion and workplace action is shaped by production imperatives. Here specialised knowledge is held within the production process itself – it is not necessary for a production line worker to develop a specialised competence but rather to follow instructions efficiently. In contrast, some occupations work almost exclusively with specialised knowledge (i.e. academic researchers), while many 'traditional professions' such as those of medicine, law and architecture are defined primarily by the forms of specialised knowledge and associated specialised practices that accompany them (Muller 2009).

However, the extent to which specialised knowledge is available within practice is subject to the socio-epistemic and institutional conditions existent within the practice. This includes the processes by which forms of specialised knowledge are recognised and utilised within the practice, and the degree to which differing practice logics may foreground or downplay the role of specialised knowledge.

Socio-epistemic conditions in the professional and vocational community

Bernstein's identifies the origin of the professional occupations through the historical sociology of knowledge, suggesting that forms of internal commitment to quality and credibility in professional work reflect disciplinary dynamics that secured scientific progress through a secular appropriation in the medieval university of the 'personal dedication' husbanded originally in the tensions between Christianity and Greek thought (Bernstein 2000, 81–86; Muller 2009). The 'origin of the professions' is thus found in a 'guarantee' that the 'inner' commitment provides for the 'outer' 'material world' (Bernstein 2000, 85). This disciplined commitment is part of assuming a professional identity

(Bernstein 2000; Beck and Young 2005), and supports the achievement and appreciation of 'outstanding work and performance' (Higgins 2003 in Hager 2011). For Bernstein (2000, 52) the 'regions' that represent forms of occupational knowledge have recontextualised knowledge from 'pure' disciplines, with the more classical professions such as medicine or engineering selecting and transforming knowledge from the physical and biological sciences in order to meet the challenges of the profession. However, it is not just propositional forms of knowledge that are 'delocated' and 'relocated' from one socio-epistemic entity to the next (Bernstein 2000; Muller 2014). Propositional knowledge and the disciplinary practices that sustain the quality of that knowledge are inextricable (Winch 2010; Muller 2014). As Winch (2010) points out, forms of occupational and disciplinary knowledge contain various admixtures of propositional knowledge (know-that), inferential and procedural knowledge (know-how) and acquaintance knowledge, and those forms of know-how imply particular procedures for judging truth claims that must be shared and at least partially agreed at the level of the professional or vocational practice.

Thus many professional or vocational communities can be said to be recontextualisating forms of practice, at least in terms of approaches to knowledge, that have their origins in disciplinary communities, carrying with them commitments to maintaining 'integrity' and 'legitimacy' (Bernstein 2000, 86). This is not necessarily true, however, for all occupations. Bernstein's discussion of the 'generic' (2000, 52) indicates how certain non-disciplinary modes of organisation (often of a Taylorist form) can be sponsored to wrestle control of a professional or vocational field from a community underpinned by disciplined modes. We can see this, for example, in how narrow competency based approaches have been extended into the qualifications of graduate-level occupations (Jones and Moore 1993), or in attempts to reduce the academic content within school-teachers professional qualifications (Beach and Bagley 2013; Hordern and Brooks 2023). Within communities or amongst stakeholders, there may be contests between those who value recontextualised disciplinary knowledge and those who seek to indiscriminately venerate all forms of practice connected with the occupation as the source of professional or vocational knowledge, irrespective of the knowledge that underpins that practice. On the other hand, workplace knowledge and activity may mirror or reflect aspects of industrial processes, as may be the case with factory operatives or warehouse workers, and thus there is little recourse to any disciplinary knowledge. This is not to deny the value of shared 'workarounds' and useful strategies that may develop amongst workers in any workplace.

The discussion above, rooted in Bernstein's work, foregrounds the connections between knowledge, practice and professional commitment, and resonates with a normative, MacIntyrean view of practice. Professional and vocational practices may achieve what Hager (2011) describes as 'a balance' of MacIntyrean internal and external goods, entailing the conditions that are 'vital for the ongoing flourishing of the practice' (554). This 'balance' can also be thought of in terms of a particular relationship, a form of connection between the 'internal' and 'external', whereby all goods whether internal or external are inextricable from the 'purposiveness' of the practice. In some professions and vocational occupations the 'external' achievement of status or wealth may be overriding objectives for practice participants, with internal goods (such as commitments to excellence irrespective of material gain, or voluntary contributions and service to the community) either divorced from the achievement of the external goods or non-existent. Alternatively, internal goods of commitment to standards of excellence may be strong currents within a practice, and exemplified in the external realisation of that practice (Hager 2011, 555). Thus the external realisation of medical and architectural practices (in terms of completed buildings or patients healed and cared for) is directly influenced by the particular substance of internal goods, and by implication can be undermined when those internal goods are undermined.

In professions and vocations underpinned by specialised knowledge, judgements and actions that may appear 'situated' or highly contextual to the observer are often products of a broader framework of reasoning that guides decision-making and action-taking (Abbott 1988; Shalem 2014; Winch et al. 2015). Initiation within this practice, and access to the forms of reasoning therein, starts to make these judgements explicable. If systematically organised disciplinary knowledge is valued, then practitioners who engage with this knowledge will develop an enhanced technical and situated capability within the practice (Winch 2010; Winch et al. 2015) – they understand the reasoning for the actions they perform and when to adapt and adjust within parameters to achieve best outcomes. The internal goods of the practice thus guide, and become manifested within, contextual action. Winch et al. (2015) discuss how this works for teaching by identifying how involvement in a research-rich culture of professional development enhances the technical and craft knowledge needed for professional judgement and action in teaching – practitioners employ techne and phronesis reflectively, drawing appropriately on the broader propositional knowledge base with awareness of the validity and appropriacy of that knowledge to the case in hand. Similarly, Shalem's (2014) work illustrates how a teacher's 'ability to discriminate a moment worthy of attention' (94) is built upon a conceptually-derived 'ordering principle' (94) that enables teachers to understand the complexity of educational contexts through a specialised lens.

Institutional conditions

Professional and vocational practices are also shaped by norms and routines which emerge from institutions and organisations, and these may be to a greater or lesser extent entwined with internally derived and husbanded standards of excellence constitutive of the practice. MacIntyre (2007) draws attention to the role of institutions in sustaining practices, and in potentially jeopardising the 'ideals and creativity of the practice' and undermining the 'co-operative care' of its 'common goods' (194). Hager (2011) notes that for the 'actual flourishing of the practice' institutions and practice need to 'be closely integrated' (553), suggesting that the 'corrupting power' that MacIntyre (2007, 194) attributes to institutions is somewhat overblown. Organisational or institutional imperatives can, however, substantially conflict with those of practices, and where these are underpinned by different logics there are likely to be difficulties. The strength of a practice with substantive internal goods that are recognised in the external performance of the practice will require certain kinds of institutional or organisational forms to support the performance of that practice. We see distinctive forms of institutions (i.e. universities, barristers chambers, or hospitals) historically supporting the practices of particular professions in a manner that is 'closely integrated' and allows the external realisation of the internal goods of the practice. However, these institutions may be pushed as a consequence of government policies, market influence or technological development to make changes to their organisational routines and norms in ways that can be seen as compromising the practices that are enacted within them.

Thus organisational routines, rules and norms are an alternative axis around which workplace practice, or elements of workplace practice, may be structured. Knowledge of organisational routines may be highly specific to the organisation, or may reflect similar routines and processes in play in multiple organisations across a sector, all conforming to particular logics that reflect a professional, highly bureaucratic or flexible orientation. The logic that underpins the routine or rule, and the extent to which these are conformed with and enforced, may also reflect the prominence of network and interpersonal knowledge within the organisation. For some organisations, for example in forms of consultancy or in small business, it is often participation within a particular network where forms of local knowledge are shared about market opportunities that is important (see Muzio et al. 2011 for a discussion of this in terms of recruitment consultancy), and this form of knowledge may well take a pre-eminent role in forms of practice which lack strong internal goods. In Bernstein's terms these forms of fluid unstructured network knowledge are instances of horizontal discourse which is 'local', and 'context-dependent' (Bernstein 1999) and therefore ephemeral. They have value to those who are engaged within them at that time, but are 'consumed by the context' (Bernstein 2001) within which they are enacted or performed. This should not be confused, however, with forms of professional community knowledge that are held and iterated within a framework of disciplined practice that generates internal goods. In such cases this knowledge is employed in the pursuit of the realisation of the practice – the network or community itself comprises specialist practitioners who are sharing knowledge in the pursuit of the goods of their practice.

Differentiating between these forms of practice matters for novice and experienced practitioners alike when they are exposed to the complex admixtures of knowledgeability found in workplaces. A work placement or initial period of workplace learning can provide considerable insight into patterns and priorities in workplace practice, supporting the knowledge already acquired in educational institutions or introducing practitioners to how that knowledge is extended or reworked within practice contexts. However, how what Billett (2006) terms the 'workplace curriculum' is organised and ordered has considerable bearing on whether opportunities for new knowledge and insight are recognised and taken by practitioners. As Winch (2010) notes, forms of acquaintance with practice are vital for the development of vocational expertise, but access to the forms of practice that enable that expertise may be variable. Workplace learning sits within meso-level productive systems (Felstead et al. 2009) that influence what is considered valuable knowledge. Those in workplaces may be offered the discretion and control of their own work activities necessary to extend their knowledge and competence, but these may also be suppressed or marginalised by managerial process (Eraut and Hirsch 2007). Equally, some may have opportunities to experience and explore workplace practice in other organisations, and the profile of practice 'affordances' or opportunities to learn may vary or be similar across organisations within a given sector, with implications for the extent to which opportunities to learn outside the 'home' workplace are beneficial (Fuller and Unwin 2004; Billett 2006).

Summarising specialised and non-specialised elements of professional and vocational knowledge and practice

Having established the rationale for differentiating forms of knowledge, and how this differentiation interconnects with the differentiation of practice, it is useful to provide a brief summary of forms of professionally and vocationally relevant knowledge and associated practices, differentiating between the 'specialised' and 'non-specialised'. This is not intended to be an attempt to exhaustively list all forms of professional and vocational knowledge and practice, but rather to emphasise the nature of differentiation and specialisation. 'Specialised' forms exist within systematic or partially systematised architectures of knowledge, or are products of such architectures, in which the value and purpose of those elements of knowledge therein is constituted via inferential relations (Winch 2014; Young and Muller 2016). In contrast 'non-specialised' forms have no such obvious systematisation, even though they may be organised locally for specific purposes related to particular contexts (i.e. the taxi driver 'knowledge' outlined by Barnett 2006). Inevitably in much professional and vocational education and practice the various forms or knowledge are inter-mingled within curricula, pedagogy, judgement and action, and therefore distinguishing between them empirically is often problematic.

As Muller (2014) identifies building on Winch (2010), it is problematic to overstate the role of explicit propositional knowledge in practice based on Bernstein's (1999) work, and yet to overstate tacit forms without acknowledging first the role of systematic explicit knowledge is also problematic (Winch 2010). Systematic knowledge forms incorporate elements of 'know-how' which may be partially tacit, although it can reasonably be argued that tacitness should be made explicit wherever reasonably possible in order to make knowledge accessible to potential practitioners seeking to join the occupational community. Similarly, non-specialised forms are not exclusively tacit by any means, as may include organisational procedures and policies, or local geographical knowledge that is explicit but yet specific to a context.

Specialised professional and vocational knowledge forms and associated practices

These could be said to include:

i propositional knowledge or 'know-that' that is nested within an architecture of concepts that are connected via inferential relations (Young and Muller 2016, 170) – this know-that is part of a disciplined structure – an 'applied discipline' in the case of occupationally relevant knowledge (Winch 2010).

ii inferential know-how and the practice of this know-how – or 'the ability to grasp and employ such inferences' (Winch 2013, 132) that relate to the propositional knowledge above.

iii procedural know-how and the practice of this know-how – or the ability to 'distinguish between claims which can be counted as knowledge and those which count as true beliefs' (Winch 2013, 132).

iv aspects of principled and procedural knowledge which is specialised to the purposes of that practice (Young and Muller 2014; Young and Muller 2016) – in some occupations this may be absorbed within category (i) above, fuelling the ongoing development of knowledge production of the occupation.

v specialised acquaintance knowledge (a subset of Winch's (2010, 2013) acquaintance knowledge), which might include acquaintance with aspects of judgement and action that is informed by specialised know-that (i) and know-how (ii and iii): specific practice contexts may afford access to this knowledge by acquaintance, and it may be reinforced through observation, conversation and reflection – it is a form of knowledge that requires engagement with specialised forms of practice.

vi diagnostic frameworks that enable practitioners to make judgements – these sit at the interface of systematic knowledge and practice but are bounded and structured by the conceptual underpinnings of the knowledge base (Abbott 1988; Shalem 2014): the greater the systematisation of the knowledge base the more structured and bounded the diagnostic framework becomes, and the more specialised the 'lens' with which the practitioner views, and engages within, the practice context.

vii knowing how to participate in the practice community: the employment of (i), (ii), (iii), (iv), (v) and (vi) is underpinned by forms of participation that are specialised to the occupation – this participation may include involvement in forms of appraisal and review; the identification and refinement of standards of excellence; appreciation of the external realisation of the professional or vocational practice; development of criteria to evaluate claims to expertise (Addis and Winch 2019); disciplined articulation of problematics or practice; and commitment to sustaining the practice through supporting new practitioners – i.e. through mentoring – these are in essence 'specialised elements of the practice' that enable its ongoing activities.

These knowledgeable forms could be said to approximate to a professionally or vocationally orientated version of Bernstein's (1999) 'vertical discourse', but importantly, as noted above, they need to be sustained by a balance or relationship between the internal goods and the external realisation of the practice (Hager 2011) and by an appropriately supportive institutional framework that holds individual organisational and market logics in check, and enables the identification of the problems of practice and the sourcing and recontextualising of appropriate disciplinary knowledge (Barnett 2006; Hordern 2014a).

Non-specialised professional and vocational knowledge and practice

This amounts to various elements of what could be described, drawing on Winch (2010) as non-specialised occupational propositional knowledge, know-how and acquaintance knowledge, much of which is gained through practice.

i propositional knowledge specific to an organisation or workplace (for example this may be organisational policies or procedures)

ii forms of practical know-how specific to organisation and workplaces, and the practice of using that know-how

iii certain forms of personal knowledge – these may be 'rules of thumb' or ways of enacting practical activity that could, potentially, become 'specialised' if articulated with, and evaluated against the existing body of specialised knowledge outlined above (Muller 2014; Young and Muller 2016), and providing the rules exist within the occupational community to evaluate such claims.

iv forms of procedural knowledge specific to governmental policies, regulations and perhaps to employer representative bodies, where this is not derived from specialised knowledge.

v   network knowledge gained from exchange of information between those involved in an occupational practice.
vi knowledge relating to a particular locale or geographical area (i.e. Barnett's (2006) taxi driver knowledge).

The practices that relate to these non-specialised knowledge forms are characterised by their specificity, and are driven and affected by economic circumstances, technological change and market values. The limitations on their usefulness beyond local and time-limited contexts calls into question the extent to which they should be incorporated extensively in a programme of professional or vocational education and training.

Concluding remarks

How practices are realised in specific organisations and workplaces also matters, although the extent to which these practices are themselves differentiated depends on the extent to which the specialisation of the professional or vocational practice permits variation in local organisational and workplace practices. The range within which expansiveness and restrictiveness (Fuller and Unwin 2004) can vary within a sector or occupation may relate to the character of specialisation in the sector or occupation (Felstead et al. 2009), while its parameters are also substantially shaped by the political economy of work. The environments within which medical practitioners learn must by their nature be sufficiently expansive to enable the development of expertise, whereas human resource practitioners, or even university researchers on fixed-term contracts, may enjoy varying levels of expansiveness in different organisations which view their contributions differently. What is different here is that medicine is an occupation enjoying a distinct specialisation and requirements for specialised knowledge underpinned by professional and legal frameworks. Thus employing organisations of medical practitioners are under greater pressure to provide the requisite expansive experience of practice. On the other hand, human resource practice has a more limited underpinning specialisation, and thus employing organisations have greater freedom to shape practice experiences.

The emphasis on differentiating practice in terms of underpinning specialised knowledge, purposiveness and supporting institutions thus has implications for how professional and vocational education and training are conceived. What appears as situated and contextual is often bounded and framed within a specialised systematic structure. Aspects of a doctor or teacher's tacit knowledge may be highly specialised, providing the socio-epistemic infrastructure exists to sustain that specialisation as outlined in Hordern (2014a, 2014b). Accessing such expertise is, however, only possible through interrelating forms of specialised propositional knowledge, know-how and acquaintance with knowledge use in practice. For such specialised occupations, immersion in practice alone is insufficient if expert capability is required.

Differentiating those aspects of practical experience that support the development of specialised expertise and identifying how novice practitioners can be best guided so that they acquire that expertise, within an overall programme structure that ensures that relevant systematic knowledge is related to those experiences, is thus key for assembling programmes of professional and vocational education.

References

Abbott, A. (1988). *The System of Professions: An essay on the division of expert labour.* Chicago: University of Chicago Press.

Addis, M. & Winch, C. (2019). Introduction. In M. Addis and C. Winch (eds) *Education and Expertise.* Chichester: Wiley, pp. 1–20.

Allais, S. (2012). 'Economics imperialism', education policy and educational theory, *Journal of Education Policy*, 27 (2), 253–274.

Barnett, M. (2006). Vocational knowledge and vocational pedagogy. In M. Young and J. Gamble (eds) *Knowledge, Qualifications and the Curriculum for South African Further Education.* Pretoria: Human Sciences Research Council, pp. 143–157.

Beach, D. and Bagley, C. (2013). Changing professional discourses in teacher education policy back towards a training paradigm: A comparative study. *European Journal of Teacher Education* 34 (4), 379–392.

Beck, J. and Young, M. (2005). The assault on the professions and the restructuring of academic and professional identities: A Bernsteinian analysis. *British Journal of Sociology of Education*, 26 (2), 183–197.

Bernstein, B. (1999). Vertical and horizontal discourse: An essay. *British Journal of Sociology of Education*, 20 (2), 157–173.

Bernstein, B. (2000). *Pedagogy, Symbolic Control and Identity* (revised edition). New York: Rowman & Littlefield.

Bernstein, B. (2001). From pedagogies to knowledges. In A. Morais, I. Neves, B. Davies and H. Daniels (eds) *Towards a Sociology of Pedagogy: The contribution of Basil Bernstein to research.* New York: Peter Lang, 363–368.

Billett, S. (2006). Constituting the workplace curriculum, *Journal of Curriculum Studies*, 38(1), 31–48.

Billett, S., Harteis, C. and Gruber, H. (2014). *International Handbook of Research in Professional and Practice-Based Learning.* Springer: Dordrecht.

Clark, L. and Winch, C. (2004). Apprenticeship and applied theoretical knowledge. *Educational Philosophy and Theory*, 36 (5), 509–521.

Cook, D. and Chatterjee, P. (2015). *Our Changing World: Let's be ready.* London: RICS.

Eraut, M. and Hirsh, W. (2007). *The Significance of Workplace Learning for Individuals, Groups and Organisations.* Cardiff: SKOPE.

Felstead, A., Fuller, A., Jewson, N. and Unwin, L. (2009). *Improving Working as Learning.* London: Routledge.

Foray, D. and Hargreaves, D. (2003). The production of knowledge in different sectors. *London Review of Education*, 1 (1), 7–19.

Freidson, E. (2001). *Professionalism: The third logic.* Cambridge: Polity Press.

Fuller, A. and Unwin, L. (2004). Expansive learning environments: Integrating organizational and personal development. In H. Rainbird, A. Fuller and A. Munro (eds) *Workplace Learning in Context.* London: Routledge, pp. 126–144.

Furlong, J. (2013). *Education: An anatomy of the discipline. Rescuing the university project.* London: Routledge.

Jones, L. and Moore, R. (1993). Education, competence and the control of expertise. *British Journal of Sociology of Education,* 14 (4), 385–397.

Hager, P. (2011). Refurbishing MacIntyre's account of practice. *Journal of Philosophy of Education* 45 (3), 545–561.

Hanrahan, H. (2014). The evolution of engineering knowledge. In M. Young and J. Muller (eds) *Knowledge, Expertise and the Professions.* Abingdon: Routledge, pp. 109–127.

Hordern, J. (2014a). How is vocational knowledge recontextualised? *Journal of Vocational Education and Training,* 66 (1), 22–38.

Hordern, J. (2014b) Regions and their relations: Sustaining authoritative professional knowledge. *Journal of Education and Work,* 29 (4), 427–449.

Hordern, J. and Brooks, C. (2023). The core content framework and the 'new science' of educational research. *Oxford Review of Education,* 1–19. https://doi.org/10.1080/03054985.2023.2182768.

Kemmis, S., Wilkinson, J. Edwards-Groves, C. Hardy, I., Grootenboer, P. and Bristol, L. (2014). *Changing Practices, Changing Education.* Singapore: Springer.

MacIntyre, A. (2007). *After Virtue: A study in moral theory.* Notre Dame, IN: University of Notre Dame Press.

Moore, R. (2007). *The Sociology of Knowledge and Education.* London: Continuum.

Muller, J. (2009). Forms of knowledge and curriculum coherence. *Journal of Education and Work* 22 (3), 205–226.

Muller, J. (2014). Every picture tells a story: Epistemological access and knowledge, *Education as Change,* 18 (2), 255–269.

Muzio, D., Hodgson, D., Faulconbridge, J., Beaverstock, J. and Hall, S. (2011). Towards corporate professionalisation: The case of project management, management consultancy and executive search, *Current Sociology,* 59 (4), 443–464.

Nicolini, D. (2013). *Practice Theory, Work and Organisation: An introduction.* Oxford: Oxford University Press.

Rouse, J. (2001). Two concepts of practices. In T.R. Schatzki, K. Knorr-Cetina and E. Von Savigny (eds) *The Practice Turn in Contemporary Theory.* Abingdon: Routledge, pp. 189–198.

Rouse, J. (2007). Social practices and normativity. *Philosophy of the Social Sciences,* 37 (1), 46–56.

Schatzki, T. (2001). Introduction: Practice theory. In T.R. Schatzki, K. Knorr-Cetina and E. Von Savigny (eds) *The Practice Turn in Contemporary Theory.* Abingdon: Routledge, pp. 1–14.

Schatzki, T. (2010). *The Timespace of Human Activity. On performance, society and history as indeterminate teleological events.* Lanham, MD: Lexington.

Shalem, Y. (2014). What binds professional judgement: The case of teaching. In M. Young and J. Muller (eds) *Knowledge, Expertise and the Professions.* Abingdon: Routledge, pp. 93–105.

Wheelahan, L. (2007). How competency-based training locks the working class out of powerful knowledge: A modified Bernsteinian analysis, *British Journal of Sociology of Education,* 28 (5), 637–651.

Wheelahan, L. (2010). *Why Knowledge Matters in Curriculum.* London: Routledge.

Winch, C. (2010). *Dimensions of Expertise: A conceptual exploration of vocational knowledge.* London: Continuum.

Winch, C. (2013). Curriculum design and epistemic ascent. *Journal of Philosophy of Education* 47 (1), 128–146.

Winch, C. (2014). Know-how and knowledge in the professional curriculum. In M. Young and N. Muller (eds) *Knowledge, Expertise and the Professions*. Abingdon: Routledge, pp. 47–60.

Winch, C., Oancea, A. and Orchard, J. (2015). The contribution of Educational Research to Teachers' professional learning – philosophical understandings, *Oxford Review of Education*, 41 (2), 202–216.

Young, M. (2006). Conceptualising vocational knowledge: Some theoretical considerations. In M. Young and Gamble, J. (eds) *Knowledge, Curriculum and Qualifications for South African Further Education*. Cape Town: HSRC Press, pp. 104–124.

Young, M. (2007). *Bringing Knowledge Back In: From social constructivism to social realism in the sociology of education* (1st edn). Abingdon: Routledge.

Young, M. and J. Muller. (2007). Truth and truthfulness in the sociology of educational knowledge. *Theory & Research in Education*, 5 (2), 173–201.

Young, M. and J. Muller (2013). On the powers of powerful knowledge, *Review of Education* 1 (3), 229–250.

Young, M. and Muller, J. (2014). Towards the sociology of professional knowledge. In M. Young and J. Muller (eds) *Knowledge, Expertise and the Professions*. Abingdon: Routledge, pp. 3–17.

Young, M. and Muller, J. (2016). *Curriculum and the Specialisation of Knowledge-* Abingdon: Routledge.

7

KNOWLEDGEABLE PRACTICE AND TEACHING

Introduction

In a paper that discussed changes in teacher education in Sweden and England, Beach and Bagley (2013) drew on Bernstein's (1999) notion of a horizontal discourse to explain the incursion of notions of the 'everyday' into discourses relating to teaching. This horizontal 'everyday' knowledge is contrasted, in Bernstein's (1999) paper, with more systematically structured disciplinary-based 'vertical' discourse. An examination of Bernstein's work on knowledge structures can underpin an exploration of the types of knowledge that inform professional practice (Young and Muller 2014), but foregrounding the differentiated nature of knowledge that Bernstein outlined poses challenges for how professional practice is conceptualised. This has particular resonance for teaching and teacher education. Reforms in England and Sweden (Beach and Bagley 2013), and pressures on teacher education internationally to meet educational policy objectives (Tatto 2006) have given impetus to new models of teacher professional formation that challenge the role of educational institutions in providing abstract conceptual knowledge for teaching, suggesting instead that teachers can acquire requisite expertise through forms of 'practice immersion' and extensive practical experience in school (Maandag et al. 2007).

For example, in England from 2010 onwards we have seen the initiation and development of the School Direct model, which places responsibilities for teacher education on schools. School Direct has been promoted as a more 'relevant' mode of formation based on the assertion that 'the classroom', in contrast to the university, is always 'the best place for teachers to learn as well as to teach' (Gove 2013). More recently (between 2019 and 2022), we have seen further reforms to teacher education, via the DfE-led market review (DfE 2021) and the

DOI: 10.4324/9781003054474-9

introduction of the Core Content Framework (CCF), that have challenged the role of universities in teacher education and attempted to foreground the role of school-led organisations. Similar challenges to the role of universities in determining the knowledge base for teaching are posed by planned reforms to teacher education in Australia (Australian Government 2023). Such reforms and initiatives are often based on the supposition that novice teachers can acquire the most useful forms of teaching expertise through direct experience of teaching practice while learning centrally mandated content, a model influenced by views of teachers as 'technicians' whose role it is to implement prescribed curriculum and pedagogy (Tatto 2006; Winch 2014).

This chapter sets out to examine in greater depth the relevance of Bernstein's 'vertical' discourse for teacher formation, its relation to horizontal discourse, and how these concepts provide insight into the nature of teachers' knowledge and practice. Teacher formation is understood here as the processes by which teachers develop expertise and assume a professional identity, as I outlined in (Hordern 2014a) and (Hordern 2022). Drawing on the work of Winch (2010) and Young and Muller (2014) on expertise, in addition to aspects of Bernstein's (1999, 2000) work on the sociology of knowledge, this chapter develops a conception of teaching as a specialised or knowledgeable professional practice that need to be supported by particular social arrangements and conditions embedded in communities of professionals. Improvements in teaching quality, and ultimately educational outcomes, can thus only be made if certain conditions are developed and sustained within a professional community of teachers and teacher educators, broadly understood.

Bernstein's discourses and their relevance to teacher formation

Beach and Bagley (2013) identify the resurgence of a 'training paradigm' in teacher education, outlining how Bernstein's (1999) vertical and horizontal discourse distinction provides a useful means for delineating between the types of knowledge prioritised in teacher education. Beach and Bagley argue that the 'context-bound, specific, concrete' nature and 'common sense knowledge' (2013, 387) of horizontal discourse has increasingly dominated teacher education in England, and to a lesser extent in Sweden, at the expense of the 'theoretical and abstract' (387) vertical discourse that provides a better foundation for professional knowledge. They suggest that the horizontal discourse provides a 'very poor basis for developing thoughtful practice, as it runs against the idea of a teaching profession grounded on scientific research-based "know-why" knowledge' (387–388), while vertical discourse 'in the form of a robust system of concepts and practices' (388) is necessary 'to describe, model and theorise from empirical situations to help students in and after teacher training to understand the ideological and political restructuring that is going on around them' (388) and 'as a tool for analysing trends and thinking critically and strategically about teaching and learning processes' (388).

There is no doubting the clarity of the distinction that Bernstein (1999) makes between vertical and horizontal discourse, a distinction with its origins in Durkheim's between the 'sacred' and the 'profane' (Young 2009; Young and Muller 2014). Vertical discourse has a number of characteristics that delineate it from horizontal discourse. Specifically, it has a 'coherent, explicit, and systematically principled structure', which is 'hierarchically organised, as in the sciences' or comprises 'a series of specialised languages with specialised modes of interrogation and specialised criteria for the production and circulation of texts, as in the social sciences and humanities' (Bernstein 1999, 159). It is these aspects of structure and specialisation which enable vertical discourses to act as the repositories of valuable disciplinary knowledge, shaping the knowledge iterated and refined by past generations and providing the criteria by which new knowledge claims can be judged. Horizontal discourse, in contrast, is 'oral, local, context dependent' (159) and therefore ephemeral or particular to individuals, unable to provide any basis for value estimation outside of its immediate context. Horizontal discourse is 'circulated' through a process of 'tacit recontextualising' which relies on the maximisation of 'encounters with persons and habitats' (159), suggesting the importance of personal contact in the relevant context, whereas vertical discourse is distributed through 'explicit recontextualisation and evaluation', enabling knowledge to be reviewed and iterated through transparent mechanisms. Vertical discourse corresponds to the structure of the academic disciplines and, for Bernstein, forms a starting point for the constitution of professional knowledge (2000, 52).

However, when approaching issues of professional knowledge, education and learning, a number of factors come into play that somewhat complicate issues discussed above. Bernstein differentiated between the academic disciplines or 'singulars' (2000) and the more professional or vocationally orientated 'regions', which lie at the 'interface between disciplines (singulars) and the technologies they make possible' (Bernstein 2000, 52). 'Singulars' and 'regions' can be construed as socio-epistemic entities which are useful in analysing how knowledge develops in academic and professional fields through the interrelation between knowledge structure and social forces (Muller 2009; Young and Muller 2014). In 'singulars' (i.e. disciplines such as maths or history) academics use disciplinary procedures to establish and iterate the knowledge base with regard only to the requirements of the discipline itself. Singulars are reasonably tightly 'bounded' or 'classified', enabling them to conserve and iterate the unique properties of their discipline and its unique vertical discourse. However, in a 'region' (i.e. medicine or engineering) those involved in establishing and iterating the knowledge base must have regard to the requirements of professional practice as much as the existing professional disciplinary body of knowledge. The broader range of stakeholders with interests in the work of the profession can complicate the process of establishing and iterating the body of professional knowledge.

The process of the development of a 'region' requires a 'recontextualisa-tion' of singulars for the 'supervening purpose' of practice (Muller 2009, 213), suggesting that one or more singular vertical discourses may be 'selec-ted', 'appropriated' and 'transformed' (i.e. recontextualised) by a 'recontex-tualisation principle' that serves to 'constitute its own order' (Bernstein 2000, 33) in the region. While Bernstein did not use teaching as an example, the mention of other professional fields such as 'medicine' and 'engineering' sug-gests that 'education' and its professionals can reasonably be construed as a region, with implications for how vertical discourse and its relation to hor-izontal discourse are understood. Indeed, work that has developed Bernstein's work for understanding professional knowledge and expertise has included studies of the teaching profession (Shalem 2014; Taylor 2014), and highlights the 'region' as central to analysis of the constitution of expertise (Young and Muller 2014, 13–15).

Key questions for understanding professional knowledge, therefore, include how a body of specialised knowledge is recontextualised from vertical dis-courses, whether and how this knowledge acquires and maintains 'verticality', and how professional practice 'in the field' is underpinned by this knowledge. Relatedly, it is important to establish which 'singular' disciplinary vertical dis-courses provide for a given knowledge base, and how elements of these dis-courses are selected. Drawing on Winch's (2010, 2014) and on Muller (2014), this specialised knowledge could be said to consist both of proposi-tional 'know-that' and inferential and procedural 'know-how', in addition to forms of acquaintance knowledge that enable the development of expertise. Arguably, considering the engagement with diverse contexts which char-acterises professional work, it is also important to develop an understanding of the relation between specialised professional knowledge and the horizontal discourses of the everyday. While certain elements of practical and particular knowledge may be inextricable from a given specialised body of knowledge (Winch 2014), many professionals have to work within contexts over which they have only limited control. In other words, professionals do not work in a vacuum, and are subject to a range of social and political influences. In Bern-stein's (1971, 2000) terms the classification 'insulation', or strength of boundaries, between professionals' specialised knowledge and practice and wider 'practices' within the world in which they work is weaker than in the case of the 'pure' production of academic knowledge, and the nature of this 'boundedness' varies from profession to profession. Professionals require the knowledge schema that enable 'diagnosis' of cases (Abbott 1988; Shalem 2014), meaning that the professional knowledge base must take account of the complexity and contextuality encountered in practice, and yet links must be sustained and iterated with a more distant abstract theoretical base of 'dis-tinctive concepts' so that solutions can be developed to unforeseen problems arising in professional work. While horizontal discourse(s) may play only a marginal role in processes of professional judgement, these may enable understanding of the complexity in which professionals work and the efficacy of professional action (as discussed in Chapter 4).

In the case of teaching, it could be argued that a number of notions of vertical discourse are at work underpinning specialised teaching knowledge and practice. A teacher, particularly working in a secondary, and sometimes a primary, phase is very often a 'subject specialist' and therefore could be considered, at least partially, working within and drawing on the vertical discourse of the subject that they teach. Of importance here is consideration of Noddings's (2003) distinction between the 'maths teacher' and the 'mathematician', and whether they both, despite their distinct specialist roles, could be seen as part of a practice called 'maths', which, we could argue here, is constituted from a pure 'singular' vertical discourse. However, the 'maths teacher' is perhaps also drawing on another specialised body of knowledge underpinned by vertical discourse, that of 'pedagogy' or 'didactics' (perhaps in some continental European contexts). Of course, the extent to which this body of pedagogical knowledge is seen as a 'professional discipline' or non-academic 'nonsense', as was asserted by the Social Affairs Unit in England in the 1980s (Anderson 1982), depends on the socio-political context and the nature of the professional 'region', and may be rather different across different nation states. Whereas the constitution and ongoing iteration of a discipline of 'pedagogy' or 'educational sciences', despite change to structure and assumptions, maintains some salience for teacher education in Sweden (Beach and Bagley 2013), and indeed in various forms across Europe (Alexander 2004), in England this is called into question.

The policies towards teacher education advocated by the coalition government in England, at least during the period of time that Michael Gove was secretary of state for education (2010–2014), suggest that the academic subject provides sufficient 'vertical' discourse for teaching practice, and indeed that any 'educational' specialist discourse has the potential to be counterproductive for teaching (i.e. Gove 2013). Such assertions challenge the notion of teaching as a specialised practice, suggesting a 'subject specialist' and 'craft' model, with teaching practice specific to subjects best learnt through experience and contact with more experienced practitioners from that subject (see also Furlong and Whitty 2017 on liberal education and craft models). While learning from experienced teachers may be an important part of professional development for the novice teacher, the denigration of academic pedagogy risks allowing all manner of pedagogical techniques to gain prominence. In other words, we are left with a form of subject-based specialism that may be coupled with forms of horizontal discourse, as context specific techniques and 'local' practices are foregrounded. This may be particularly the case if pedagogies championed by powerful independent educational organisations aspiring to growth are not subjected to scrutiny.

While the subject specialist debate has particular relevance at secondary level, in primary education the notion of the generalist class teacher has a strong influence in many countries, in Europe and internationally (Le Metais 2003). This suggests a lesser role for the vertical discourse that underpins school subjects, and potentially a much greater role for a pedagogical or didactical vertical discourse. Indeed, a high proportion of primary teachers in England have historically studied three-year education-related degrees (Furlong 2013), and primary teacher education in many European countries often consists of strongly didactically orientated undergraduate or master's-level programmes (Zuljan and Vogrinc 2011) that would seem to require engagement with specialised discourse specific to education.

For example, in Norway, recent reforms require all primary and lower secondary teacher education programmes to 'switch to five-year integrated master's level programmes that combine enhanced knowledge and research competency with inquiry-rich school experiences' (Cochran-Smith 2021, 18). As Cochran-Smith (2021) outlines, the reform process explored the role and professional knowledge of teachers in the primary and lower secondary phase in a detailed and rigorous process of consultation and enquiry, resulting in the lengthening and deepening of professional preparation. Furthermore, Maria Teresa Tatto and I, commenting on a comparative study of maths teacher education, demonstrated the salience of national pedagogical traditions in teacher education programmes in Germany, showing the influence of 'long-standing traditions of educational theory and pedagogy' (Tatto and Hordern 2017, 266). In the same study, teacher education programmes in Poland were shown to maintain a 'widespread commitment to covering philosophy of education' (265). Some teacher preparation programmes therefore continue to require a distinctive vertical educational discourse, and this may well be a reflection of national traditions (Furlong and Whitty 2017).

The structure of professional knowledge is significant for the nature of professional identity and the capacity to generate trust and confidence in professional judgement, and therefore for the future sustainability of the profession. For Bernstein, as it was for Durkheim (Grace 2014), and for Abbott (1988) and Freidson (2001), the specialised nature of professional work necessitates the *disciplined* production of conceptual knowledge that has relevance across a range of practice contexts, and this implies the importance of research activity in higher education institutions that can continually produce and iterate vertical discourse. Without a specialised vertical discourse underpinning professional practice, professional identity is unbounded and flexible, ready to be bent towards the whims of government or the market (Freidson 2001; Beck and Young 2005). In Bernstein's (2000) terms, specialised discourse provides strong boundaries which enable practitioners to recognise the nature of their practice and their role within it, leading to a specialised professional identity that can be acknowledged, and trusted, by clients of the profession and the general public. Equally, if practice itself is not shaped and constrained by the underlying conditions provided by a disciplined discourse, then professional judgement is open to influence by various fads and untested techniques.

Recontextualisation for specialised professional practice

The processes by which knowledge is selected, appropriated and transformed for practice (i.e. recontextualised) are particularly important for the
constitution of professional knowledge. Building on Bernstein's work,
Barnett (2006, 147) describes a process of 'reclassificatory recontextualisation' as vertical discourses are transformed to become a 'toolbox of
applicable knowledge' that is designed to address the problems of practice.
However, this reclassification is only possible if the 'technological and
organisational problems' (Barnett 2006, 148) of practice are defined and
framed in a way that disciplinary knowledge can be selected and appropriated to aid in their solution. However, the definition of problems for
practice is often a complex political and social negotiation between parties
interested in the work of the profession. In teaching, for example, we have
seen considerable interest from governments concerned that the 'definition
of problems' is not monopolised by teachers themselves or their representatives. In England, we have seen struggles between government, the
unions, academics and the teaching profession around the role of teachers
and the core purposes of education (Furlong et al. 2000; Beck 2008), and
Beach and Bagley (2013) indicated some similar tensions emerging in
Sweden. The problems of teaching practice can be variously defined as
relating to improving exam results, improving behaviour and discipline,
extending opportunities to all, and ensuring pupils are well prepared for all
aspects of their future lives. How these problems are accented and framed
has considerable impact on what types of knowledge are considered
appropriate for teacher formation.

The situation in England contrasts furthermore with that in Scotland
where there appears to be a greater consensus around the purpose and
character of schooling and the role of teachers (Menter and Hulme 2011),
and indeed more recently also with Wales (Furlong et al. 2021), leading
perhaps to a more settled definition of the 'problems of practice'. The idea
of the recent reforms to curriculum and teacher education in Wales, where
they have specifically sought to build on and learn from the experience of
reform in Scotland, is to bring government, universities and school together
around a shared agenda, using extensive and rigorous processes of consultation and engagement. In Wales the outcome in terms of teacher education
has been a plan that requires 'schools and universities … to work closely
together in the conceptualisation, in the management and in the teaching' of
teacher education programmes and to hold partners 'jointly accountable for
the quality of provision' (Furlong et al., 2021, 64). The Welsh reforms
acknowledge that addressing the 'problems of practice' that underpin the
professional knowledge of teaching requires the complementary contributions of schools and universities in recontextualising knowledge for teaching
and shaping the teacher education programmes of the future.

The process of defining 'problems' is also framed by how practice itself is conceptualised. If teaching practice is conceived as routine, requiring levels of judgement and decision-making that are relatively easy to acquire, then an argument can be made that problems are straightforward and can be simply met through the provision of suitable knowledge resources, packaged appropriately for the practitioner. However, if teaching practice is considered as requiring forms of conceptuality that can help teachers make 'good sense' of the variety of contexts which they encounter (Winch et al. 2015), with new challenges and problems constantly arising and complex processes of professional judgement and decision-making required, then a more specialised knowledge base is needed which supports the development of the capability of individual teachers, so that they can infer, assess and act confidently cognisant of the implications of their actions (Guile 2010; Winch 2010). How a practice is conceived has a considerable impact on what processes are used to define problems, and who is considered sufficiently capable of engaging in the process of definition. From conservative or 'traditionalist' perspectives, education is too important to be left to 'progressive educationists' (Campaign for real education, 1999), suggesting that problems must be defined and solved outside of a professional community of teaching, leaving it to teachers merely to implement solutions in a linear and unproblematic manner. Alternatively, teachers understanding and awareness of their own practice can be considered a fundamental resource within the definition of educational problems, and thus a key contributor to the 'reclassificatory recontextualisation' (Barnett 2006) of knowledge for teaching.

Recontextualisation is, at root, a process by which knowledge is 'selected', 'appropriated' and 'transformed' for a new context (Bernstein 2000; Barnett 2006), but in terms of professional learning this process can be seen as occurring at a variety of levels, including those of knowledge production, validation, curriculum, pedagogy, workplaces and by the learners (professionals) themselves (Evans et al. 2010; Guile 2010; Hordern 2014b). It is also important to note that processes of recontextualisation are influenced by the socio-historical context of the profession and its societal role, which may differ by nation and by historical period, and may be shaped by transnational conceptions of the profession, agreements between professional associations, or more formal legislative or institutional factors, as I outlined in Hordern (2014b, 2014c, 2021). The esteem and value that is attributed to the profession in a given context may also support the profession in mitigating external pressures, including from other professions and government (Abbott 1988).

In what ways can teaching practice be considered 'specialised'?

The sociology of the professions posits that specialisation emerges where types of work require particular forms of knowledge and preparation (Abbott 1988; Freidson 2001), where work demands conceptualisation that is not readily available to the uninitiated. Complex work that is considered particularly valuable for society becomes specialised, driven forward by public backing for the generation of knowledge that fuels greater professional awareness of different conditions or circumstances. The process of specialisation requires categorisation, and the development of norms and conditions that can assure the public of the value of the work, a 'normative structure' (Winch 2010, 80) that symbolises rigour and quality. Questions of whether teaching should be specialised labour are inextricable from questions about the extent to which education is considered important for society and involving complex thought and action. While education itself 'cannot compensate for society' (Bernstein 1970) it has enormous influence on the formation of individual identities, with teachers having the capacity to make a considerable impression on student enthusiasm for different academic subjects and to influence processes of socialisation.

It is clear, however, that at least in England there is considerable variability in the ways in which education is considered important, and in the role of the teacher in providing that education. The growth in supra-national measurement and increasing political interference in schooling has resulted in assessed performance of pupils in standardised tests dominating evaluation of the worth of education, with impacts on how teacher education is shaped and structured (Tatto 2006). Education is often seen purely in service to the economy as a result of the dominance of ideologies that see investment in 'human capital' as the key to economic growth (Lauder et al. 2012), with the consequence that the 'internal goods' (MacIntyre 2007) of education are marginalised as the most powerful focus only on what is measurable, in particular qualification achievements and test performances. The teacher's role is often seen as that of implementer of policies and initiatives, with little meaningful to contribute apart from efficiency, competence and industry. In such circumstances 'specialisation' in teaching is considered minimal, with professional judgement implicated as a routine process.

It is important to consider what certain prevalent conceptions of the nature of teaching mean for concepts of specialisation. As Winch et al. (2015) identify, both the notion of the teacher as a craftsman/woman and the teacher as a 'technician' have particular resonance in England, and have variable levels of influence on policy developments in teacher education in other countries, for example in Sweden (Beach and Bagley 2013) and indeed across Europe (Zuljan and Vogrinc 2011). In the craft conception of teaching, the teacher primarily learns through experience in the workplace, with expertise acquired through practice. In some versions this mode of learning is described as an 'apprenticeship', although how this is conceptualised and occasionally denigrated by critics working in the field of teacher education perhaps overlooks theoretical development in studies of vocational learning (e.g. by Guile and Young 1998 or Fuller and Unwin 2004). Craft conceptions of teaching often venerate models of communities of practice, drawing on Lave and Wenger

(1991) or others. Experience in the workplace is central to such models when applied to professional formation, and yet there is a risk that the limitations for learning of certain types of workplace experience are not sufficiently acknowledged (Fuller et al. 2005). The craft conception is often coupled with the view of the teacher as a 'subject specialist', as discussed above. Here, there is specialisation through the subject community, but if this is allied with 'learning on the job' without encouraging a 'good conceptual grasp of education, including its contestable elements' (Winch 2012, 313) then teachers cannot adequately interpret and make judgements about knowledge developed through educational research, or about suggestions for new curricular or pedagogical strategies.

The craft conception also risks a prioritisation of knowledge on the basis that it is preferred by an organisation or by dominant voices within a particular hierarchy, with limited scope for entertaining the possibility of alternative perspectives. In a teaching context, one can see the potential for particular institutions immersing new 'craft' teachers in particular teaching practices favoured in those institutions without developing the teacher's capacity to acquire, and to critique, other teaching practices. An 'immersive' school-based teacher education model could lead to teaching experiences outside the host school being afforded little value, and this may be exacerbated by reforms that place greater power in the hands of chains of schools as noted in Hordern (2014a). Knowledge in such scenarios can be highly 'specific' to context, and not necessarily specialised, if there is no link with the processes and procedures validated by society as appropriate for specialisation. As Winch et al. (2015) have identified, the craft conception of teaching is sceptical of the value of educational research, and indeed implies that there is no requirement for research into practice at a *systemic* level. While research into professional learning is clear on the value of learning from others in workplaces (e.g. Fuller and Unwin 2004; Eraut 2007), what may be missing in the 'craft' conception of teacher formation is an adequate recognition of the importance of institutions and social relations for arbitrating the value of knowledge and expertise, as will be discussed further below.

The view of the teacher as 'technician' is equally problematic for the notion of specialisation. In this conception, 'what works' in education is established at a systemic level by policy-makers or curriculum authorities, and teachers are then tasked with implementing pre-packaged parcels of effective practice, expressed in terms of curriculum or pedagogical techniques, to meet prescribed outcomes. There is some tension here between a technician with a degree of autonomy and discretion, and what Winch terms the 'Executive Technician' (2010, 165). While the reasonably autonomous technician is less constrained and has scope to develop their expertise, the executive technician is charged to 'execute a precept derived from someone else' (165). Certainly, an emphasis on the teacher as technician allows for teaching to become in some sense 'specialised', but the specialisation of the knowledge is held at some distance from the teachers themselves (Hordern 2022).

In the technician model teachers are not encouraged to understand *why* knowledge has been specialised in a particular way and to contribute to the ongoing review and development of its specialised nature. Instead, teachers are only encouraged to become experts in *how* to teach on the basis of that specialised knowledge, so to authoritatively implement practices specified for them by governments and their agencies. In the terms outlined above, knowledge is recontextualised (selected, appropriated and transformed) for the teachers at a 'safe distance' by governments who do not enable (or trust) those teachers to develop the capability to recontextualise knowledge for themselves. The distance between teachers and the organisers of teacher knowledge has multiple implications, as the pre-specified knowledge and the requirements for its implementation may be in considerable tension with the realities of the contexts in which teachers work. The insights that teachers inevitably gain within workplace practice are accorded limited value, and teachers are not included within discussions about the relevance and appropriacy of the curricula and pedagogies they are asked to implement. Arguably there are echoes of this approach in the recent introduction of a 'Core Content Framework' for initial teacher education in England (DfE 2019), which specifies a narrow knowledge base for teaching that is centrally prescribed (Hordern and Brooks 2023).

In summary, prevalent conceptions of teaching practice as related to craft or (executive) technical models are problematic at a variety of levels. They tend to absolve or disempower teachers from the development of their own professional capability and a deeper understanding of contexts in which they work (and use of research is often considered irrelevant to practice). The exclusion of bodies of educational theory means that teachers may have difficulty in conceptualising the complexity of human interaction and processes of learning within the contexts that they encounter (Winch 2012, 315), and difficulty in conceiving of hypothetical new contexts that may extend their conceptualisation of alternative forms of practice. The craft and technician notions negate the importance of the capacity for inference in professional judgement (Winch 2010), and suggest that teachers need 'no conceptual grasp of education' (Winch 2012, 313), leaving teachers at a loss in the face of new challenges for which they have not been prepared.

The technician notion in particular suggests that teachers cannot be trusted to make sound well-reasoned professional judgements (and yet following the arguments above must be trusted because of the importance of the role). Whereas the craft notion restricts the horizon of professional formation, and naively assumes that individual practitioner experience alone is a sufficient model for expertise. This neglects the role of quality mechanisms in all disciplines and professions for establishing the 'truth', 'truthfulness' and 'fitness for purpose' of professional knowledge (Young and Muller, 2007, 2014; Muller 2009). Neither does the craft of executive technician models recognise the sociality of knowledge production or the need for certain conditions to be met for knowledge to acquire validity, as will be discussed below. The models also overlook the significance of enabling teachers to organise (recontexualise) their own knowledge in order to develop professionally.

Maintaining the socio-epistemic conditions for specialised professional teaching practice

For teaching to enhance its specialisation and professionalism the arguments above suggest that there are both 'social' and 'epistemic' conditions that need to be met. The inadequacy of prevalent conceptions of teaching practice is coupled with weak conceptions of teaching knowledge. This is unsurprising if one considers how our understandings of professional knowledge have become dominated by an over-emphasis on any kind of 'practice' as a source of knowledge (Young and Muller 2014). As Bernstein's work demonstrates, there are structural differences between specialised vertical discourses and the contextually limited horizontal discourses that relate to their inherent epistemic character and quality, and to the social relations that support their development. Practice can indeed be specialised, and potentially also a source of knowledge, but surely only if underpinned by recontextualised forms of vertical discourse that provided the epistemic structures that enable practitioners to make judgements about the value of current and new knowledge for the purpose of that practice (see also my argument in Hordern 2022).

It is important to conceptualise the conditions for specialisation as 'socio-epistemic' (Muller 2009; Young and Muller 2014). For Young and Muller (2013), drawing on the previous work of Young (2009) and Moore (2007) and with roots in that of Bernstein (1999, 2000), specialised knowledge should be 'systematically revisable' (Young and Muller 2013, 236) and 'emergent', and thus ever-changing, although 'originating contexts may leave their mark on the knowledge', with 'criterial rules for acceptability' acting as a process through which knowledge is revised, discarded and re-admitted to the knowledge base (237). Specialised knowledge is 'produced in particular socio-epistemic formations' (238), as 'disciplines differ in terms of their internal material cultures' (238). Underlying this argument is the assertion that 'specialised knowledge is real' and 'material and social', and therefore there is the implication that knowledge can acquire a degree of objectivity, but also that all knowledge is fallible and may be improved through further research and enquiry. While much of this thinking, at least in Bernstein's work (1999), was originally applied to academic disciplines, there is no doubt that the same principles have resonance for professional knowledge (Young and Muller 2014), albeit through a process of 'recontextualisation' (Bernstein 2000, 52).

For a specialised professional practice to be sustained, therefore, the social relations need to exist within the professional community that generate and maintain the 'criterial rules', and a stance on knowledge that accepts its 'fallibility' but nevertheless the potential for a degree of objectivity, always keeping in mind that knowledge bears the imprint of those who were involved in its production. Those professional 'regions' that have close relations or are highly 'proximate' (Hordern 2014c) to academic disciplines draw on the latest disciplinary developments but also often mirror these academic disciplines in the application of procedures and principles for the appropriation and transformation of knowledge for practice. Medicine is a paradigmatic example, requiring a particular admixture of professional 'know-that' and concomitant specialised 'know-how' from its practitioners, but also sustaining the procedures, principles and 'criterial rules' of a discipline, albeit one with a distinctly professional orientation.

In England, the reforms initiated by the coalition government to school organisation and governance and teacher education from 2010 onwards make the development of these social relations highly problematic. This can be contrasted with Scotland, for example, where a greater systemic cohesiveness, the central involvement of higher education in teacher education and a greater commitment to finding agreements (Menter and Hulme 2011) provides a better basis for these social relations to emerge. Major contrasts between the two countries exist around forms of professional association, as evidenced by the differing roles and fates of the respective General Teaching Councils, but also in the success of initiatives such as union learning representatives in Scotland (Alexandrou and Davies 2006) which demonstrate the potential of integrating practitioners in teaching improvement/professional development strategies.

Specialisation of teaching knowledge and practice, underpinned by the social relations outlined above, enables recontextualisation agents (i.e. professional associations, higher education institutions, teacher educators and teachers) to appropriate, select and transform vertical discourses to provide a knowledge base for teaching. As noted above, the involvement of teachers in the definition of problems is important, but this also needs reframing in conversation with researchers in higher education, in order for extant bodies of knowledge to be brought to bear on those problems. The two specialised discourses of the disciplinary background and educational/pedagogical research are recontextualised to provide pedagogical knowledge for teaching, at least for secondary teachers. At primary level, recontextualisation relies to a greater extent of the educational/pedagogical research, and the elements of knowledge recontextualised are slightly different, given the more 'generalist' formulation of the role of the primary teacher.

Teaching needs to be a specialised knowledgeable professional practice because professional practice cannot function without specialised knowledge (Abbott 1988; Freidson 2001). Specialised knowledge must be conceptual and revisable (Winch 2010; Young and Muller 2013), and education as an activity is too important for society to not be specialised, given its central societal role (Bernstein 2000; Biesta 2010). While, internally at least, the conditions for this are achievable, there can be no doubting the difficulties involved considering the ways in which governments are keen on using education instrumentally, to achieve specified objectives which articulate uneasily with long-held societal and professional conceptions of education and its practice.

References

Abbott, A. (1988). *The System of Professions: An essay on the division of expert labour.* Chicago: University of Chicago Press.

Alexander, R. (2004). Still no pedagogy? Principle, pragmatism and compliance in primary education, *Cambridge Journal of Education*, 34 (1), 7–33.

Alexandrou, A. and Davies, J. (2006). Union Learning Representatives – a new source of professional support for Scottish teachers. *Research in Post-Compulsory Education*, 11 (2), 175–190.

Anderson, D. (1982). *Detecting Bad Schools: A guide for normal parents.* London: Social Affairs Unit.

Australian Government (2023) *Strong Beginnings: Report of the Teacher Education Expert Panel.* Canberra: Australian Government.

Barnett, M. (2006). Vocational knowledge and vocational pedagogy. In M. Young and J. Gamble (eds) *Knowledge, Qualifications and the Curriculum for South African Further Education.* Pretoria: Human Sciences Research Council, pp. 143–157.

Beach, D. and Bagley, C. (2013). Changing professional discourses in teacher education policy back towards a training paradigm: A comparative study. *European Journal of Teacher Education*, 34 (4), 379–392.

Beck, J. (2008). Governmental professionalism: Re-professionalising or de-professionalising teachers in England. *British Journal of Educational Studies*, 56 (2), 119–143.

Beck, J. and Young, M. (2005). The assault on the professions and the restructuring of academic and professional identities: A Bernsteinian analysis. *British Journal of Sociology of Education*, 26 (2), 183–197.

Bernstein, B. (1970). Education cannot compensate for society. *New Society*, 15 (387), 344–347.

Bernstein, B. (1971). On the classification and framing of educational knowledge. In M. Young (ed.) *Knowledge and Control: New directions for the sociology of education.* London: Collier Macmillan, pp. 47–69.

Bernstein, B. (1999). Vertical and horizontal discourse: An essay. *British Journal of Sociology of Education*, 20 (2), 157–173.

Bernstein, B. (2000). *Pedagogy, Symbolic Control and Identity* (revised edition). New York: Rowman & Littlefield.

Biesta, G. (2010). *Good Education in an Age of Measurement: Ethics, politics, democracy.* Boulder, CO: Paradigm.

Campaign for Real Education (1999). The traditional and progressive philosophies of education. http://www.cre.org.uk/philosophies.html.

Cochran-Smith, M. (2021) *Rethinking Teacher Education: The trouble with accountability, Oxford Review of Education*, 47 (1), 8–24.

Department for Education (DfE) (2019). ITT core content framework. London: DfE. https://www.gov.uk/government/publications/initial-teacher-training-itt-core-content-framework.

Department for Education (DfE) (2021) Initial Teacher Training (ITT) Market Review. London: DfE. https://www.gov.uk/government/publications/initial-teacher-training-itt-market-review.

Eraut, M. (2007). Learning from other people in the workplace. *Oxford Review of Education*, 33 (4), 403–422.

Evans, K., Guile, D., Harris, J. and Allan, H. (2010). Putting knowledge to work. *Nurse Education Today*, 30 (3), 245–251.

Freidson, E. (2001). *Professionalism: The third logic*. Cambridge: Polity Press.

Fuller, A., Hodkinson, H., Hodkinson, P. and Unwin, L. (2005). Learning as peripheral participation in communities of practice: A reassessment of key concepts in workplace learning. *British Educational Research Journal*, 31 (1), 49–68.

Fuller, A. and Unwin, L. (2004). Expansive learning environments: Integrating organizational and personal development. In H. Rainbird, A. Fuller and A. Munro (eds) *Workplace Learning in Context*. London: Routledge.

Furlong, J. (2013). *Education: An anatomy of the discipline. Rescuing the university project*. London: Routledge.

Furlong, J., Barton, L., Miles, S., Whiting, C. and Whitty, G. (2000). *Teacher Education in Transition: Re-forming professionalism?*Buckingham: Open University Press.

Furlong, J., Griffiths, J., Hannigan-Davies, C., Harris, A. and Jones, M. (2021) The reform of initial teacher education in Wales: From vision to reality, *Oxford Review of Education*, 47 (1), 61–78.

Furlong, J. and Whitty, G. (2017). Knowledge traditions in the study of education. In G. Whitty and J. Furlong (eds) *Knowledge and the Study of Education: An international exploration*. Didcot: Symposium, pp. 13–57.

Gove, M. (2013). Michael Gove speaks out about the importance of teaching. Speech at Policy Exchange, London, 5 September.

Grace, G. (2014). Professions, sacred and profane. In M. Young and J. Muller (eds) *Knowledge, Expertise and the Professions*. Abingdon: Routledge, pp. 18–30.

Guile, D. (2010). *The Learning Challenge of the Knowledge Economy*. Rotterdam: Sense.

Guile, D. and M. Young (1998). Apprenticeship as a conceptual basis for a social theory of learning. *Journal of Vocational Education and Training*, 50 (2), 173–193.

Hordern, J. (2014a). The logic and implications of school-based teacher formation. *British Journal of Educational Studies*, 62 (3), 231–248.

Hordern, J. (2014b.) How is vocational knowledge recontextualised? *Journal of Vocational Education and Training*, 66 (1), 22–38.

Hordern, J. (2014c). Regions and their relations: Sustaining authoritative professional knowledge. *Journal of Education and Work*, 29 (4), 427–449.

Hordern, J. (2021). Recontextualisation and the teaching of subjects. *Curriculum Journal*, 32(4), 592–606. https://doi.org/10.1002/curj.110.

Hordern, J. (2022). Specialized educational knowledge and its role in teacher education. In I. Menter (ed.), *The Palgrave Handbook of Teacher Education Research*. London: Palgrave Macmillan, pp. 1–18. https://doi.org/10.1007/978-3-030-59533-3_14-1.

Hordern, J. and Brooks, C. (2023). The core content framework and the 'new science' of educational research. *Oxford Review of Education*, 1–19. https://doi.org/10.1080/03054985.2023.2182768.

Lauder, H., Young, M., Daniels, H., Balarin, M. and Lowe, J. (2012). Introduction. In H. Lauder, M. Young, H. Daniels, M. Balarin and J. Lowe (eds) *Educating for the Knowledge Economy? Critical Perspectives*. London: Routledge, pp. 1–24.

Lave, J. and Wenger, E. (1991). *Situated Learning: Legitimate peripheral participation*. Cambridge: Cambridge University Press.

Le Metais, J. (2003). *International Trends in Primary Education*. London: Qualifications and Curriculum Authority.

Maandag, D.W., Deinum, J.F., Hofman, W.H. and Buitnik, J. (2007). Teacher education in schools: An international comparison. *European Journal of Teacher Education*, 30 (2), 151–173.

MacIntyre, A. (2007) *After Virtue: A study in moral theory* (3rd edn.) Notre Dame, IN: University of Notre Dame Press.

Menter, I. and Hulme, M. (2011). Teacher education reform in Scotland: National and global influences. *Journal of Education for Teaching*, 37 (4), 387–397.

Moore, R. (2007). *The Sociology of Knowledge and Education*. London: Continuum.

Muller, J. (2009). Forms of knowledge and curriculum coherence. *Journal of Education and Work* 22 (3), 205–226.

Muller, J. (2014). Every picture tells a story: Epistemological access and knowledge. *Education as Change*, 18 (2), 255–269.

Noddings, N. (2003). Is teaching a practice? *Journal of Philosophy of Education*, 37 (2), 241–251.

Shalem, Y. (2014). What binds professional judgement: The case of teaching. In M. Young and J. Muller (eds) *Knowledge, Expertise and the Professions*. Abingdon: Routledge, pp. 93–105.

Tatto, M.T. (2006). Education reform and the global regulation of teachers' education, development and work: A cross-cultural analysis. *International Journal of Educational Research* 45 (4–5),231–241.

Tatto, M.T. and Hordern, J. (2017). The configuration of teacher education as a professional field of practice: A comparative study of mathematics education. In G. Whitty and J. Furlong (eds) *Knowledge and the Study of Education*. Didcot: Symposium, pp. 255–274.

Taylor, N. (2014). Knowledge and teacher professionalism: The case of mathematics teaching. In M. Young and J. Muller (eds) *Knowledge, Expertise and the Professions*. Abingdon: Routledge, pp. 171–184.

Winch, C. (2010). *Dimensions of Expertise: A conceptual exploration of vocational knowledge*. London: Continuum.

Winch, C. (2012). For philosophy of education in teacher education. *Oxford Review of Education* 38 (3), 305–322.

Winch, C. (2014). Know-how and knowledge in the professional curriculum. In M. Young and J. Muller (eds) *Knowledge, Expertise and the Professions*. Abingdon: Routledge, pp. 47–60.

Winch, C., Oancea, A. and Orchard, J. (2015). The contribution of educational research to teachers' professional learning – philosophical understandings. *Oxford Review of Education*, 41 (2), 202–216.

Young, M. (2009). Education, globalisation and the 'voice of knowledge'. *Journal of Education and Work*, 22 (3), 193–204.

Young, M. and Muller, J. (2007). Truth and truthfulness in the sociology of educational knowledge. *Theory & Research in Education*, 5 (2), 173–201.

Young, M. and Muller, J. (2013). On the powers of powerful knowledge. *Review of Education*, 1 (3), 229–250.

Young, M. and Muller, J. (2014). Towards the sociology of professional knowledge. In M. Young and J. Muller (eds) *Knowledge, Expertise and the Professions*. Abingdon: Routledge, pp. 3–17.

Zuljan, M.V. and Vogrinc, J. (eds) (2011). *European Dimensions of Teacher Education: Similarities and differences*. Ljubljana: University of Ljubljana.

8

KNOWLEDGEABLE PRACTICE, POWERFUL KNOWLEDGE AND THE CURRICULUM

Introduction

The notion of 'powerful knowledge' (hereafter PK) (Young and Muller, 2013, 2016; Muller and Young, 2019) has had an impact in both academic circles and in the domains of educational policy and practice and has been used as a justification for a subject-based curriculum. In England, the reforms of the Conservative-led coalition government of 2010–2015 shifted the national curriculum in a 'knowledge-based' direction, and PK has become an inspiration for 'knowledge-led' curriculum change in schools in England (Counsell, 2018). The revised school inspection framework in England, and the research supporting its development, has focused extensively on subject knowledge in the curriculum (Ofsted, 2018), and the Chartered College of Teaching (CCT), the new professional body for teachers in England, have highlighted PK within their publications for teachers (CCT, 2018). Conservative politicians have been particularly enthusiastic, identifying a 'knowledge-based' curriculum as aligned with a focus on improving pupil assessment outcomes and a 'driver of true meritocracy' (Gibb, 2017). Policymakers have increasingly identified PK as a 'curriculum principle' (Carlgren, 2020, 323), using it as a basis to justify curriculum interventions in schools. However, Young has exposed the differences between the arguments for PK and those of the conservative politicians (Young, 2011, 2015), and it is questionable whether contemporary curriculum interpretations of PK adequately reflect the underpinning arguments for PK in the sociology of educational knowledge, as I have argued previously (Hordern, 2019). Meanwhile, substantive work has been done to articulate the implications of PK for school subjects such as History and Geography, and influenced the thinking of subject specialists and educationalists internationally, including in countries such as Sweden, Australia and South Africa (Nordgren 2017; Maude 2018; Bertram 2019).

DOI: 10.4324/9781003054474-10

While PK has enjoyed a growing impact in schools and in some policy circles, and amongst some subject-focused curriculum thinkers it has met
increasing critique from sociologists, curriculum theorists and philosophers of
education. Zipin, Fataar and Brennan (2015) were amongst the first to
articulate a challenge, arguing that PK's focus on disciplinary knowledge
offered an inadequate basis for social justice through the curriculum, while
White (2018) has provided criticism of various conceptual aspects of PK.
Recurrent criticisms include those that argue that PK is epistemologically
unsound (Wrigley 2018; Alderson 2020), misunderstands the nature and
value of experience (Wrigley 2018), and demonstrates a lack of attention to
power differentials and disadvantage (Zipin, Fataar and Brennan 2015;
Rudolph, Sriprakash and Gerrard 2018). Curriculum scholars such as Carlgren (2020) and Deng (2020) have provided recent engagement. Carlgren
(2020) has suggested that PK is constrained by its rationalism and Cartesian-
ism and needs to engage to a greater extent with social practice theory, suggesting that PK should be rethought as powerful knowings and knowns.
Deng (2020), while remaining supportive of elements of PK, suggest that PK
needs rethinking with closer engagement with *Bildung*-centred *Didaktik* and
Schwab's work in order to support the development of content that will be
meaningful in teaching contexts.

This chapter provides a further illustration of the applicability of notions of
knowledgeable practice, with our attention turned here to curriculum studies.
It is argued that the work on PK can be usefully reconsidered in the light of
the idea of knowledgeable normative practice (Rouse 2007), as this provides
for a fuller understanding of processes and accountabilities which are not discussed in the PK thesis, and offers a more incisive grasp on the relation
between knowledge, knowing and experience. In contrast to Carlgren's
(2020) advocacy of the 'practice turn' in social theory, it is argued that greater
engagement with normative and 'less attenuated' (Hager 2013) conceptualisations of practice can explicate what is distinctive about how PK is
constituted and recontextualised. Drawing on the work of (inter alia) Rouse
(2007), MacIntyre (2007) and Dunne (2005), it is argued that powerful
knowledge is sustained by normative specialised and knowledgeable practices
that are defined by shared purposes, mutual accountability, prospectivity and
the generation of practice 'goods'. Notions central to the PK thesis, such as
systematic revisability and the role of specialised communities (Young and
Muller 2013) can thus be more fully understood via the idea of (normative)
knowledgeable practice. The argument has implications for how the work of
teachers as recontextualisers of disciplinary knowledge and shapers of the
subject curriculum is understood, and for how the curriculum is conceptualised in terms of the relation between knowledge and experience. The
chapter therefore complements the two other chapters in this part of the book
(Chapters 6 and 7) which focus on illustrating the applicability of notions of
knowledgeable practice in professional education and teaching.

Unpacking knowings and knowns

In a recent paper critiquing PK, Carlgren argues for a 'shift in focus from the knowns to the knowings' and a 'widening of the concept of knowledge … to also include the tacit aspects' (2020, 324). Carlgren makes the persuasive argument that much of what constitutes knowledge is 'invisible', like an iceberg beneath the surface (324), implying that curriculum thinkers such as Young and Muller (2013) are mistaken to focus solely on the explicit propositional knowledge which is visible, tangible and can be expressed in curriculum documents and text books. According to Carlgren, PK is guilty of carrying a 'ballast of Cartesian, rationalist thinking' and gives 'priority to theory over practice with propositional knowledge as the most valuable and a foundation for good practical action' (2020, 324). The 'conceptual pile' therefore takes on a 'godlike appearance' (328), which relegates or renders invisible the purposeful practical action that could be seen as a constituent element of any subject. Carlgen draws on Wittgenstein in arguing that 'practice is a necessary prerequisite for knowledge' (326), highlights Polanyi's 'relational view of knowledge' (327) and discusses Paul Hirst's 'troubled rationalism' and 'practice turn' (328–330). In so doing, Carlgren argues for a shift to the 'tacit dimensions of knowledge … its embeddedness in action' and its 'practical foundation' (2020, 326), while noting that such a move does not 'replace knowledge with practice' or 'give practice a primary position in relation to theory' (327). Underpinning Carlgren's arguments is the assertion that this 'epistemology of practice' advanced by the 'practice turn in social theory' (2020, 324) has been ignored in the PK thesis, and this has resulted in an excessive focus on propositional knowledge at the expense of other aspects (on the knowns rather than the knowings). The authors of PK have therefore erroneously misconstrued the epistemology of practice by suggesting it reduces 'all knowledge to know how' and 'knowing … to doing' (Carlgren 2020, 327). 'Know-that' has thus been given underserved priority in PK, and the 'know-how' advanced by Ryle, Wittgenstein and Polanyi has been sidelined. The consequence is a devaluation of the intangible epistemological glue that holds the visible propositional elements of a discipline or subject together.

It is possible to view PK as less rationalist and Cartesian than Carlgren's (2020) interpretation. For example, Young and Muller acknowledge the arguments for inferential know-how in the realisation of meaning from accumulations of propositional knowledge (2016, 171–172). In other words, propositions and concepts can only be fully understood in relation to other propositions and concepts, and this is only possible if we know how to infer meaning in the relevant norm-governed 'space of reasons' (Derry 2018, 96; see also Young and Muller 2016, 169–170). Derry (2018), drawing on Vygotsky's work, also emphasises the 'systematic relations between concepts' (89) which provide purchase and power, remarking also that 'the existence of a concept as a living idea … results from the normative constraints within which it is articulated' (89). While Carlgren notes PK's engagement with inferentialism (2020, 328), the implications for how 'practice' might be accordingly conceptualised have not been fully elaborated, either by Carlgren (2020) or Young and Muller (2010, 2013, 2016).

The PK thesis also acknowledges the importance of what Winch (2010) calls procedural know how, in other words the processes by which new claims to knowledge are evaluated (see Young and Muller 2016, 100–101). While Carlgren (2020) also notes this, the implications in terms of the type of practice required to sustain this procedural dimension of PK are not addressed. Would such a practice be built only on 'invisible' or 'tacit' knowings, or might there be a role for more explicit criteria (Addis and Winch 2019)? Young and Muller (2013) suggest that PK is 'systematically revisable', and thus for the power of the knowledge to be sustained the practice must enact systematic revision via a specialised community with sufficient expert knowledge to make decisions. Such a view of knowledge highlights its fallibility, revisability, contingency and questionability (Young and Muller 2010, 2013), all characteristics which offer scope for a less Cartesian interpretation than Carlgren suggests, and points to the importance of specific types of practice that can underpin the processes of systematic revision and the enactment of procedures and criteria.

Young and Muller (2010) make a clear distinction between a Future 1 curriculum based upon a 'naturalised and under-socialised concept of knowledge' and a Future 3 curriculum based upon the ideas that there are 'specific kinds of social conditions under which powerful knowledge is acquired and produced' (19), suggesting that PK emerges from and is relayed within specific specialised social practices. While Oates (2018) suggested that there was considerable proximity between a Future 1 and Future 3 curriculum, Morgan, Hordern and Hoadley contend that these should be interpreted as 'strongly differentiated' (2019, 108), with PK (as represented by Future 3) 'emergent, non-reducible and socially differentiated', and socio-historically constructed through the disciplinarity of 'communities of enquirers' (Young and Muller 2010, 14). A Future 3 curriculum, which Young and Muller (2010, 2013) see as the appropriate vehicle for powerful knowledge, emphasises the historicity and evolution of knowledge, and needs also to acknowledge the socio-epistemic processes by which judgements are made about revisions to the knowledge base of any subject or discipline.

Carlgren (2020) does, however, agree with Young and Muller (2013) that the curriculum should offer something different from the 'everyday', and that schools should 'offer experiences of a different kind than pupils can have in everyday life', and 'not least important is the experience of theoretical work' (333). Zipin et al. might thus interpret Carlgren's position as aligned with Young and Muller's (2013) 'deficit view' of the lifeworld (Zipin, Fataar and Brennan 2015, 19), drawing a clear boundary between the school and the everyday life of students. But Carlgren's (2020) emphasis is on a broader conception of knowledge which derives from a practice-based understanding, as opposed to the (assumed) over-emphasis on propositional or conceptual knowledge in the PK arguments. Carlgren's argument is that curriculum thinking should start with 'the practice-based theories of knowledge' which can stipulate 'how the everyday world differs from disciplinary and other expert worlds, which in turn differ from each other', and stipulates that 'specific kinds of practices are necessary for the development of specific powerful ways of knowing' (2020, 333). However, Carlgren does not outline the characteristics of a 'disciplinary' or 'expert world' as opposed to an 'everyday world', or discuss the processes by which any activity within such expert worlds would be established as an appropriate performance of the expertise. And yet such processes and characteristics would be central to the formulation and enactment of a curriculum based on such principles. How, therefore, can we differentiate between specialised and non-specialised (everyday) practices, if such a distinction is possible?

Yet there is a further important question which Carlgren's (2020) arguments pose. If 'practice is a necessary prerequisite for knowledge' (and those practices may be expert, disciplinary and specialised), then to what extent can knowledge 'emerge' from those practices and have resonance in other related (or possibly unrelated) practices? The claim that PK is 'emergent' is central to Young and Muller's (2013) arguments, and by this they mean that PK is 'produced by social conditions and contexts but cannot be reduced to them' (2013, 237), while 'criterial rules for acceptability' and the 'social norms' (237) of disciplinary practices are important for evaluating claims to emergence. However, the notion of emergence and a degree of independence from context also suggests that knowledge may take a pathway independently of the (specialised) practice that produced it. Specialised knowledge may prove useful in new contexts separated in time and space from its original context of production, as for example in the case of Greek thought in the early modern period (Valleriani 2014). However, what is needed when (powerful, emergent) knowledge is brought into a new practice is the capacity to 'select', 'appropriate' and 'transform' (or recontextualise) this knowledge so that it meets the purposes of the new practice in which it is to play a role. The explicit, tangible, knowledge is incorporated into a fresh practice and may be further recontextualised, disassembled and reassembled in order to address new problematics and concerns, a process that may nevertheless be shaped by the Wittgensteinian 'games and rules' (Carlgren 2020, 326) of the receiving practice.

If knowledge is 'emergent' it is not therefore solely dependent on the practice which produced it for its existence as it can remain 'in storage' in libraries and databases (perhaps indefinitely), but to *exercise* its power it needs to be employed within a practice to answer a problematic. While certain types of specialised practice may be needed to produce PK, and to recontextualise it for the development of curriculum and for teaching, propositional knowledge and other forms of testimony can exist semi-independently of the practices in which they were produced, and may be available for recontextualisation into different practices for different purposes. While practice may be a 'prerequisite' (Carlgren 2020, 326) for knowledge production, knowledge can also move *between* practices, and in so doing be appropriated, selected and transformed in various ways (Bernstein 2000). Moreover, the capacity for the storage, transmission and reconfiguring of knowledge since the early modern period has a considerable impact on the potential for recontextualisation, including for teachers interested in using a range of material for the teaching of subjects, as I noted in a previous article (Hordern 2021).

Differentiating subject and disciplinary practices from the everyday: the importance of normative practice

While Carlgren (2020) has importantly drawn attention to conceptualisations of practice, the 'practice turn in social theory' (Schatzki, Knorr Cetina and von Savigny, 2001) is a broad church, and there are important conceptualisations of practice that have longstanding roots that arguably *sit outside* the practice turn. It can be argued that instead of the predominant versions of the 'practice turn' there are particularly fruitful conceptualisations of subject and disciplinary practice in the 'normative' (or 'less attenuated') versions of practice (Rouse 2007; Hager 2013), as these offer explanations for how purposeful forms of expertise can be identified and sustained over time, while considering inclusivity and participation. A normative or 'less attenuated' conception of practice, as will be outlined below, offers a framework for identifying the characteristics and processes of a specialised disciplinary or subject practice, thus suggesting what could comprise a curriculum offer.

As explained in Chapter 2 of this book, practice theories fall into two principal camps located 'along a continuum', according to Hager (2013, 94–96), with conceptions of practice inspired variously by Wittgenstein, Heiddeger and Aristotle (85). In the first camp there are the 'more attenuated' versions of practice, often inspired by Wittgensteinian philosophy and its interpretation in social theory. In these versions 'practice' is often used as a 'collective term for a whole host of disparate activities' or as 'micro level human behaviours, activities or, even, actions' (Hager 2013, 95). The focus of such versions of practice could be on quite 'mundane doings' such as making phone calls or cooking a meal (Nicolini 2013, 10). Hager criticises such excessively attenuated uses of practice as 'neither particularly explanatory nor enlightening' (95), suggesting that the term is often used as a catch-all for all phenomena. While it could be argued that the attention to describing micro-level behaviours could give rise to focused and rich descriptive work, there is a risk of an absence of analytical purchase if there is no explanation for the organising principles of the practice and how activities are sustained over periods of time. Those versions of practice which have greater analytical utility, according to Hager, have at *least some criteria for what constitutes a practice*, and provide some explanation for the 'interconnectedness' of activities (2013, 95). A focus on interconnectedness could entail highlighting how mental, material, bodily and emotional states are interrelated or somehow co-dependent. Various forms of 'more attenuated' versions of practice have been very influential in organisational studies (Nicolini 2013), in some areas of social theory and in learning theory (as Carlgren 2020, 324) notes.

The second camp Hager (2013) identifies is the 'less attenuated' versions of practice, which stipulate more detailed criteria to determine what constitutes a practice, and therefore what can be identified as 'a practice' is more constrained and clearly defined. Drawing inspiration from Aristotelian thought, a less attenuated version of practice is likely to stipulate necessary constituent elements such as 'goal directed activity' (Hager 2013, 98), the generation of 'goods internal to that form of activity' and the achievement of 'standards of excellence', as in MacIntyre's (2007, 187) influential conceptualisation. MacIntyre's notion of practice can be summarised as a 'coherent, complex set of activities that has evolved cooperatively and cumulatively over time' (Dunne 2005, 368), sustained by a committed community of practitioners, a notion that Nicolini suggests 'points towards stability' (2013, 9). Such less attenuated versions of practice suggest that processes within practice are interdependent and co-related, although these processes and the standards of excellence by which they are evaluated are continuously iterating to align with the goals to which they are directed (which might be a disciplinary problematic, for example). And while the goals, goods and standards may adapt over time to a changing environment, they do so synergistically, and with the consent of the practitioners and remaining 'true to their proper purpose' (Dunne 2005, 367). A further example of a less attenuated practice is provided by Addis and Winch's (2019) sketch of a 'criterial practice', which arises through the processes of making judgements about claims to expertise, with such claims evaluated 'in relation to the aims' of the practice and to its internal goods (2019, 9).The discursive practice of judging and evaluating claims to expertise leads to criteria which need to be 'sustained by a common view about how those criteria can be applied' (Addis and Winch 2019, 8), and therefore the practice is held together by both a sense of purpose and interactions that have special resonance for practitioners as they seek to evaluate claims to expertise.

By focusing on how normative action is constituted, Rouse (2007) also differentiates between two ways of conceptualising practice that resonate with Hager's (2013) distinction. On the one hand Rouse identifies (i) regularist and regulist conceptions, which understand practice as 'exhibited regularities or presupposed rules' (2007, 48) respectively. Practices appear, therefore, where there are regular patterns of behaviour or assumptions about rules, and this might include relatively mundane activities. Rouse argues that these notions of practice do not provide a means for explaining how the 'identity' of a practice is 'maintained across multiple iterations' (47), and thus do not help explain the durability of activity over time, or why it may be held in special regard by its practitioners.

On the other hand, Rouse outlines (ii) a 'normative conception' of practice, in which a practice is 'maintained by interactions among its constitutive performances that express their mutual accountability' (2007, 48). Such a practice is bounded 'by the ways in which its constitutive performances bear on one another' (49), as any activity within the practice is undertaken somehow in response to other practice activities. Activities are accountable to each other, and thus criteria or 'standards of excellence' (MacIntyre 2007, 187) are generated within the practice to evaluate activities. However, in order for these sequences and patterns of interactivity to persist there must be something 'at issue' or 'at stake' (Rouse 2007, 50), a purpose or 'telos' which propels the practice and provides a basis for evaluating activities. But, in Rouse's conception, the nature of what is at issue, and the means of achieving it, is 'not already settled' (50). There is thus 'no agreed-upon formulation' of what is at issue, and therefore this is constantly a matter of discussion and re-formulation within the practice, with the 'definite resolution' of what is at stake 'always prospective' (50–51). Rouse thus claims that this notion of practice offers a 'more adequate understanding of normativity in terms of accountability to what is at issue' (2007, 46). Normativity is thus not defined by observable repetition of performances, or in terms of pre-suppositions, but instead in terms of the 'appropriateness' of an action or claim in the context of the purposeful activity to which it seeks to contribute.

As noted in Chapter 2 of this book and illustrated further in subsequent chapters, the normative conception that Rouse outlines has much in common with Hager's (2013) 'less attenuated' practices. Both aim to refine what is understood by 'practice' by seeking to explain what generates and sustains practice activity over time. Both also seek to explain the 'connectedness' that various authors have identified as central to conceptualisations of practice, and to distinguish their model from those notions of practice that seem all-encompassing, vague or solely descriptive. Not all human activity will qualify within Rouse's (2007) conception of normative practice, and any given practice may only demonstrate some of the characteristics outlined. However, the normative conception suggests a useful ideal type for evaluating longstanding disciplinary or professional practice, including the specialised practice of teaching (see Chapter 7 and Noddings 2003 for a discussion of the goods in teaching practice). It provides a focus on criteria, commitment to a purpose, and beneficial goods which can explain the pursuit of 'truth and truthfulness' that Young and Muller (2016) put at the heart of the quest for PK, while acknowledging fallibility and prospectivity. The characteristics and processes of normative practice also provide a means for differentiating between specialised 'disciplinary and expert worlds' and those of the 'everyday' (Carlgren 2020, 333), and thus to delineate the specialised knowledgeable practice that underpins PK and makes it possible.

Drawing on Rouse's (2007) idea of a normative practice, it is possible to delineate some 'ideal type' features that can be said to underpin knowledgeable and specialised disciplinary and subject practices, and indeed educational practice itself (Noddings 2003; Hordern 2015), reiterating some of the arguments about the relation between knowledge and practice discussed in Chapter 3 of this book. We can argue that knowledgeable practice is characterised by: (i) an 'issue' or 'something at stake', which could be the defining problems of a discipline and the pursuit of greater understanding of the world; (ii) prospectivity, which might entail emphasising truthfulness and continual challenge in the teaching of a subject as much as a belief in truth itself; (iii) mutual accountability of constitutive performances of the practice, so that inferences and claims to knowledge within a subject are made cognisant of the implications of those inferences and claims for wider understanding and the subject as a whole; (iv) criteria or standards of excellence by which the actions seeking to be performance of the practice can be judged, so that claims to knowledge can be evaluated and subject expertise identified; and (v) the commitment of those involved in the practice to its continuation (and iteration), as could be demonstrated in teacher involvement in professional associations, curriculum theorisation and debate or in ongoing academic and professional development. Claims to contribute to the practice are held to account against the practice criteria or standards of excellence (Rouse 2007; Addis and Winch 2019), necessitating specialised communities who can enact judgements cognisant of the purpose of the practice and its existing understandings.

These characteristics cumulatively enacted give rise to 'goods' generated through the (subject, disciplinary or professional) practice which may be publicly held to be of value to society. These might include the uplifting quality and social utility of public buildings (Hager 2011), informed and productive citizens (Noddings 2003), the 'formation of the full individual' and the 'cultivation of human powers' (Deng 2020, 59), 'the process of unfolding individuality by learning' (Hopmann 2007, 115), or the development of a 'communitas' in which there is a possibility for inclusion and meaningful participation of all citizens (Bernstein 2000). While the specific enactment of the characteristics of normative knowledgeable practices may differ in the history, mathematics, science, geography or design and technology curriculum, the characteristics outlined above provide a basis for determining what makes such activities knowledgeable or expert and what differentiates them from 'everyday' practices. In the practice of history teaching, for example, what is at stake is the opportunity for all children to develop 'historical consciousness' or a 'historical gaze' (Bertram 2012), with interpretations of historical events presented as prospective and open to question, while maintaining a commitment to introducing criteria by which new claims to historical interpretation can be evaluated. This gives rise to a social good which would be a commonly held historical consciousness which would inform social discourse and democratic processes within a society.

Normative knowledgeable practice as an underpinning for powerful knowledge

Following the discussion above, we can perceive how the idea of knowledgeable practice provides an underpinning for PK by specifying the characteristics of practice that can generate and sustain PK in specialised communities. Young and Muller's PK is founded on Durkheim's (2001) differentiation between the sacred and profane and its manifestation in Bernstein's (2000) work, and this provides PK with a sociological grounding as much as a prescription for the curriculum. For Young and Muller (2013) is it the intricate sociality of Durkheim's 'collective representations' shaped in specialised communities that offer a template for contemporary disciplinary knowledge and for all expert practice in society (Wheelahan 2015), as discussed in Chapter 4 of this book. The properties of PK, including its materiality, sociality, emergence from 'originating contexts' and systemic revisability (Young and Muller 2013, 236–238), represent the distinguishing features of PK as opposed to everyday non-specialised knowledge. For Young and Muller (2013) the differentiating boundaries between PK and other forms of knowledge are necessary for society to have a conversation about itself and to organise human understanding. The purpose of PK is therefore not 'knowledge for its own sake' but the sustenance of society and the discourse that is necessary for continual societal development. Claims to contribute to PK make sense if they are accountable to previous claims, if they demonstrate their commitment to the purpose of the field of inquiry and if they acknowledge their prospectivity. PK can only be sustained therefore if underpinned by a normative knowledgeable practice that stipulates the purpose for which the knowledge is generated, formulates the criteria of excellence by which claims can be judged, and ensures that claims are accountable to the existing practice and the knowledge it husbands.

The idea of normative knowledgeable practice thus provides the parameters for purposeful activities of social value through which PK can be revised so that alternatives can be envisaged and society's conversation perpetuated (Wheelahan 2015). The distinguishing features of normative practices (prospectivity, purposefulness, the generation of goods, criteria of excellence, and the accountability of claims and performances) enable a boundary to be drawn between those activities considered knowledgeable practices and those that are more ephemeral and transient (e.g. everyday habitual activities and patterns of behaviour). The idea of normative knowledgeable practice thus establishes the conditions within which collective representations (and therefore PK) can be formulated, stipulating the requirements for the 'socio-epistemic' production, revision and recontextualization of PK. The idea of knowledgeable practice makes it possible to draw boundaries between types of practice, just as the idea of PK provides for boundaries between categories of knowledge.

However, while a boundary exists between specialised normative knowledgeable practices and 'everyday' practices, this does not mean that such a boundary is impermeable or static. While some specialised practices become embedded in the fabric of societies, this does not mean they are ahistorical or universal. Durkheim's (2001) work draws attention to the changing nature of the sacred (specialised) and profane (everyday), while asserting that the boundaries between these change over time, as noted in the conclusion to Chapter 3. Societies may come to the realisation that a practice that has hitherto been understood as 'everyday' is becoming increasingly specialised as it is recognised as of particular value to society, and here processes may be enacted to 'specialise' the underpinning practice through clarifying what is at stake and determining what can be identified as an appropriate performance of the practice. Collective social experiences which may express a view of the world hitherto marginalised or ignored by society, for example the narratives of disadvantaged groups, may need to be carefully recontextualised so that their power can be relayed to the rest of society. But in such a process the criteria by which claims are evaluated may themselves need to be refined to take account of new voices and new perspectives. What is established as specialised powerful knowledge now may not be so in the future, and new knowledgeable practices may arise to meet new problematics.

Recontextualisation, revisability and knowledgeable practice

The supplementing of powerful knowledge with normative knowledgeable practice offers a more dynamic view of knowledge and practice, and their interrelation. While Carlgren (2020) makes a persuasive argument about the invisibility of much of knowledge with the analogy of the iceberg, what is omitted in her conception is Young and Muller's (2013) emphasis on the fallibility, revisability and contingency of knowledge. In other words, the structure of the iceberg is constantly being (re)constituted as new knowledge is added and older knowledge reformulated and discarded. With new discoveries or insights the iceberg may melt and freeze to acquire a new shape and structure. The disciplines and subjects are never static, unless they become moribund and float away (potentially to be rediscovered and reinterpreted by a fresh generation of explorers at a later date)!

Normative knowledgeable practice places an emphasis on the pursuit of something 'at issue' or 'at stake' in the practice 'whose definitive resolution is always prospective' (Rouse 2007, 51). Therefore, within a knowledgeable practice there will be considerable ongoing debates amongst practitioners leading to (re)definitions of the issues 'at stake' and the best means of pursuing, investigating and communicating these to others. Such normative practices are generative of 'goods' which may nevertheless undergo processes of constant change, although the rate of change may not necessarily be rapid. Some change may be stimulated by external pressures, or internal misconceptions within the practice, and lead to some cul-de-sacs which do not result in new insights. The practice is only sustained ultimately through new insights that contribute to the definition of what is 'at stake' and how it can be beneficially pursued.

This conception of knowledgeable practice represents the conditions that would be needed to underpin what Young and Muller (2010) describe as a Future 3 curriculum, in which 'there are specific kinds of social conditions under which powerful knowledge is acquired and produced' (2010, 19) sustained within 'domain-specific but increasingly global specialist communities' (20). Young and Muller (2013) have foregrounded processes of 'systematic revisability' as a defining characteristic of PK, with disciplinary communities exercising continuous judgements on new claims to knowledge and revisions to the knowledge base according to criteria of 'bestness', and different interpretations of 'bestness' 'differentially influential over the ages' (2013, 236). The continuous revision that maintains the resonance and purchase of PK is only possible if underpinned by a practice that recognises the prospectivity of the knowledge and the problematic that new claims to knowledge are seeking to address. The purpose of the practice, in terms of a shared sense that something is 'at stake' is what holds the participating practitioners together and informs the ever-evolving criteria of 'bestness' which shapes the knowledge base. If the notion of prospectivity is lost or the issue 'at stake' devalued then the knowledge will lose something of its resonance and explanatory power, and become increasingly moribund, relying on false certainties or distortions that may suit some of the 'powerful' but undermine PK. Furthermore, if particular voices or perspectives are deliberately excluded from the practice then the revision of the knowledge is undermined, and the knowledge loses power as some challenges and lines of questioning are sidelined. The practice must be inclusive and participative and must have outcomes (Bernstein 2000).

An important further point is the issue of emergence – knowledge can move between practices, but it requires a knowledgeable practice to reinterpret that knowledge. Subject practices are not necessarily congruent with disciplinary practices and may have different purposes (Yates and Millar 2016), but yet disciplinary knowledge feeds the teaching of subjects. The structure of the disciplinary knowledge and the emergent power it offers needs recognition, but this may need to be reconfigured and transformed in the making of 'content' for teaching purposes (Deng 2020). Recontextualisation to adjust disciplinary knowledge to the needs and purposes of the subject practice is a core curriculum-making activity, lying at the heart of teacher expertise. Yet the process of recontextualisation arguably requires knowledge to be selected, appropriated and transformed in accordance with a principle that is generated and sustained through the practice. The fragmented educational knowledge base and contested purposes of education found in the Anglophone world make it difficult to establish such principles, while notions of *Bildung* provide an important educational recontextualisation principle in some continental European contexts (Hordern 2021).

The subject as a knowledgeable practice can provide a framework for recontextualisation, providing the subject practice is fostered by a community with the capacity to specify its own normative purposes and develop its own standards of excellence against which claims can be judged. Communities of subject specialist teachers, supported for example through the Historical Association and Geographical Association in the UK, are vehicles through which the subject practice is defined and sustained. These subject communities are then collectively able to make judgements about curriculum reforms and educational material, reinterpreting and recontextualising disciplinary knowledge and other sources as necessary in the interests of the teaching of the subject to students (Hordern 2021). Educational material must be developed and used in a way that is accountable to the practice, acknowledging its purpose in the educational context, which may be to provide the basis for progress within the discipline, but may also have a broader societal purpose amongst other curriculum objectives (Yates and Millar 2016). The teacher would, nevertheless, need to be aware of the previous learning, children's capabilities and the purpose of using the material in order to recontextualise the material effectively.

Knowledge and experience in knowledgeable practice

The idea of normative knowledgeable practice also provides for a reconsideration of the relation between knowledge and experience in the curriculum. Carlgren (2020) draws attention to the necessity of 'specific experiences from specific kinds of practices … for the development of specific powerful ways of knowing' and argues that a 'central task of the school is to offer experiences of a different kind than pupils can have in their everyday life' (333). Carlgren makes a distinction between the attention to 'previous experiences' and the offering of 'new experiences as a foundation for the development of powerful knowings' (Carlgren 2020, 333). In foregrounding the role of experience, this position is contrasted with that of Young and Muller who instead foreground the 'conceptual pile' and the importance of theoretical knowledge (Carlgren 2020, 328).

Carlgren's emphasis on the absence of a discussion of the relationship between knowledge and experience in Young and Muller's work has something in common with the concerns of Wrigley (2018) and Zipin et al. (2015) in their criticisms of PK. Wrigley, who is supportive of some aspects of the PK argument, including its exposure of the 'technical instrumentalism' (2018, 4) that has dominated curriculum policy in England, nevertheless critiques the 'radical divorce between academic and everyday knowledge' that he perceives as central to the PK thesis, and the 'neglect of the interrelationship between sensory experience and abstract concepts' (11). Wrigley asserts that PK is seen 'almost entirely in terms of abstract concepts' leading to a 'deeply reductionist view of knowledge' (12). Zipin et al. concur with this, suggesting that the hinterland to PK offers 'a deficit view' of everyday experience 'that misses rich potentials to use life-world knowledge for curriculum learning purposes' (2015, 19). They also suggest that the thinking behind PK disputes the possibility of 'rich curricular interaction between everyday and scientific knowledge' (Zipin et al. 2015, 21), and that 'well-selected lifeworld knowledge offers depth and vitality to schooled thinking and learning' (22). Importantly, they also argue that 'both epistemological and ethical purposes are crucially relevant, and not actually separable, for curriculum knowledge selection' (22).

It is important to note that 'everyday'/lifeworld knowledge can vary considerably from person to person, and some such knowledge may be shaped considerably by experiences in families or communities. Reiss makes the important point that 'what is everyday to one student may be exotic to another' (2018, 126), by explaining how his parents taught him multiplication at home but never played any music. His 'sensory experience' (of music at least) was thus limited and influenced his engagement with music at school, but his head start in maths and the priority it was given in his home life would have blurred boundaries between his 'everyday' and the subject knowledge of maths. While music may have felt rarified and remote, mathematics would not. Reiss (2018) goes on to make the point that technology has changed what is possible in terms of exposure to specialised knowledge outside of educational or public institutions. The child with a particular interest in mechanics or in history can now access enormous volumes of material online, although it could also be argued that understanding of these is likely to be considerably enhanced via a pedagogical relationship that can facilitate a way through the maze of online resources.

The category of 'everyday experience' or 'lifeworld knowledge' can thus be misleading if considered *in opposition* to the specialised – as experience is central to all knowledgeability. Becoming knowledgeable in any discipline or subject requires some experience in certain activities (Winch 2010): knowledge by acquaintance draws from experience, and experiential knowledge can be transformative to understanding. Lifeworld knowledge may be considerably enhanced, or even transformed, through engagement with the 'collective representations' (Durkheim 2001) of the wider community, and the lifeworld knowledge may potentially contribute to the transformation or recalibration of the 'collective' view. Lifeworld knowledge can be seen from a range of perspectives, and a process of coming into dialogue with others could enable new unexpected insight. It is this juxtaposition and interrelation between collective representations and our rich experiences which is central to the enactment of the curriculum and pedagogic practice (Gamble 2014). While some experiences and some subject knowledge may maintain a degree of separation, pedagogic work is about enabling experiences to be brought into relation with subject knowledge, and for the 'everyday' to be reconsidered in specialised terms.

McCrory (2015) introduces some helpful distinctions which can help further reframe the knowledge–experience relation, by exploring the differences between a referential and an inferential approach to meaning-making. A word or phrase can both refer directly to an object or phenomenon (referentially) and can be understood as having a role within a chain of inferences which conjure particular meaning in certain contexts and for certain people. The inferentialist arguments suggest that for those who have a certain level of initiation into a knowledge domain certain phrases or ideas will resonate within that domain, whereas for the uninitiated those phrases or ideas may only refer to physical objects or phenomena: any wider meaning remains obscured. Nevertheless, the initiated are likely to be able to switch between two experiential understandings. The furniture maker *perceives* a chair differently from the child at play, although they can also see it as 'just a chair'. The astronomer understands the significance of discovering a new galaxy differently from the non-scientist, although they can both wonder at its enormity and distance from us. New academic arguments have resonance for those who have a grasp of their provenance and are aware of which other conjectures they contest. But induction into whichever forms of reasoning requires specialised experience provided through the knowledgeable practice, so that meanings can resonate in the context of their application – depending on the subject this may entail participation in debates (politics, philosophy), experimental work (chemistry, physics), field or project work (geography), or a collaborative workshop task (design and technology).

The role of experience set out here and its relation to knowledgeability in a knowledgeable practice is notably different from Carlgren's (2020) position. While it is possible to make a distinction between previous and new experiences, and between 'everyday life' and 'experiences of a different kind' (Carlgren 2020, 333) it is also true that once we are engaged within a knowledgeable practice (such as a disciplinary or subject practice) we may acquire new insight into our previous and current experiences, and actively choose to engage in specific novel experiences. New insights are *not products of the experience itself alone*, but rather products *of the practice*, and thereby part of the process of engaging with the propositional, inferential, procedural and experiential knowledge that constitutes the subject. The same events can be experienced differently depending on the degree of induction into the knowledgeable practice of the subject, whether that be history, maths or design. The role of the teacher is in providing pathways into that knowledgeable practice, through educational experiences that illustrate the knowledge of the subject in-practice, and thereby enabling young people to interpret events or propositions in different ways. Gamble demonstrates that the process of becoming a competent craftsperson, or acquiring design capability in a classroom context, is through visualisation and performance, rather than explicit pedagogical transmission (2014, 62–63), and through this process the student acquires a specialised lens through which the standards of excellence of the specialised craft practice can be recognised and achieved. The 'material item' that students are working on becomes a specialised or 'theoretical object' (2014, 64), and thus the competent designer or craftsperson starts to recognise the specialised qualities, and areas for potential improvement, in finished objects and works-in-progress. The experience of engaging in craft, and witnessing the practice and finished products of the craft practice, is understood differently depending on the level of induction into the knowledgeable practice. The 'everyday' activities of making things at home can now be seen differently, with new potential. The pedagogic practice may thus often involve making the familiar strange (Wright Mills 1959) so that objects and experiences can be interpreted differently.

Concluding remarks

This chapter has provided a further illustration of the applicability of knowledgeable practice, in this case to debates in curriculum studies, and has revealed some further dimensions of the notion. From the discussion in this chapter, it seems reasonable to assert that the process of becoming knowledgeable within a normative practice is *not* 'an end in itself' – but a 'for purpose activity' with its own self-governed norms, criteria, goods and sense that something is 'at stake', and therefore worthwhile pursuing. We become knowledgeable about fishing, craft, mathematics or history not purely to enjoy the activity or to improve ourselves, but because these are purposive practices which produce beneficial goods and outcomes for individuals and society (Bernstein 2000; MacIntyre 2007). Carlgren's charge that Young and Muller (2013) betray a 'knowledge-as-an-end-in-itself thinking' (2020, 328) is less accurate if we consider a view of disciplines and subjects as normative knowledge practices which always answer to problematics and exist to produce goods of benefit to society (Hager 2011), as could be understood via Young and Muller's (2010) Future 3.

If knowledgeable practices are constantly undergoing change to reflect the redefinition of what is at stake, then what implication does this have for the constitution and recontextualisation of PK and the role of teaching in the formation of the individual in society? Bernstein (2000) foregrounds the need for 'enhancement', 'inclusion' and 'participation' in the formulation of the 'pedagogic rights' that underpin an authentically democratic society. The challenge for normative knowledgeable practices is to ensure that they are inclusive and participative, while offering enhancement to all those engaged in the practice, as was noted in Chapter 4 on the social and organisational dynamics of practice. If such practices do not include or allow full participation, then the knowledge that they seek to iterate may become increasingly irrelevant to the rest of society as it starts to lose its purchase on social problems of concern. Additionally, it may become increasingly alien to those who feel excluded from the practice, inaccessible or not seen as meaningful for them. With the increasing complexity of disciplinary knowledge production this raises questions also for the school curriculum and how the purposes of subjects are conceived. It also highlights the recontextualising role of teachers as curriculum-makers, charged with offering possibilities for inclusion and participation and constructing curricula which do not alienate and instead provide pathways to enhancement.

References

Addis, M. and Winch, C. (2019). Introduction. In M. Addis and C. Winch (eds) *Education and Expertise*. Chichester: Wiley, pp. 1–20.

Alderson, P. (2020). Powerful knowledge, myth or reality? Four necessary conditions if knowledge is to be associated with power and social justice. *London Review of Education*, 18 (1), 96–106.

Bernstein, B. (2000). *Pedagogy, Symbolic Control and Identity*. Rev. edn. New York: Rowman & Littlefield.

Bertram, C. (2012). Exploring an historical gaze: A language of description for the practice of school history, *Journal of Curriculum Studies*, 44 (3), 429–442,

Bertram, C. (2019). What is powerful knowledge in school history? Learning from the South African and Rwandan school curriculum documents. *The Curriculum Journal*, 30 (2), 125–143.

Carlgren, I. (2020). Powerful knowns and powerful knowings. *Journal of Curriculum Studies*, 52 (3), 323–336.

Chartered College of Teaching (CCT). (2018). *Designing a Curriculum, Impact* 2. London: CCT.

Counsell, C. (2018). Taking curriculum seriously. In *Designing a Curriculum, Impact* 2. London: CCT.

Deng, Z. (2020). *Knowledge, content, curriculum and didaktik: Beyond social realism*. Abingdon: Routledge.

Derry, J. (2018). What is educationally worthwhile knowledge? Revisiting the case for powerful knowledge. In D. Guile, D. Lambert and M.J. Reiss (eds) *Sociology, Curriculum Studies and Professional Knowledge: New perspectives on the work of Michael Young*. London: Routledge, pp. 84–96.

Dunne, J. (2005). An intricate fabric: Understanding the rationality of practice. *Pedagogy, Culture and Society*, 13 (3), 367–390.

Durkheim, E. (2001). *The Elementary Forms of Religious Life*. Oxford: Oxford University Press.

Gamble, J. (2014). Approaching the sacred': directionality in the relation between curriculum and knowledge structure. *British Journal of Sociology of Education*, 35 (1), 56–72.

Gibb, N. (2017). The importance of knowledge-based education. London: UK Government. https://www.gov.uk/government/speeches/nick-gibb-the-importance-of-knowledge-based-education.

Hager, P. (2011). Refurbishing MacIntyre's Account of Practice. *Journal of Philosophy of Education*, 45 (3), 545–561.

Hager, P. (2013). Practice as a key idea in understanding work-based learning. In P. Gibbs (ed.) *Learning, Work and Practice: New understandings*. Dordrecht: Springer, pp. 85–103.

Hopmann, S. (2007). Restrained teaching: The common core of Didaktik. *European Educational Research Journal*, 6 (2), 109–124.

Hordern, J. (2015) Teaching, teacher formation, and specialised professional practice. *European Journal of Teacher Education*, 38 (4), 431–444.

Hordern, J. (2019). Exercise and intervention: On the sociology of powerful knowledge. *London Review of Education*, 17 (1), 26–37.

Hordern, J. (2021) Recontextualisation and the teaching of subjects. *The Curriculum Journal*, 32(4), 592–606.

Maude, A. (2018). Geography and powerful knowledge: A contribution to the debate. *International Research in Geographical and Environmental Education*, 27 (2), 179–190.

MacIntyre, A. (2007). *After Virtue: A study in moral theory.* Notre Dame, IN: University of Notre Dame Press.

McCrory, C. (2015). The knowledge illusion: Who is doing what thinking? *Teaching History* 161, 37–47.

Morgan, J. Hordern, J. and Hoadley, U. (2019). On the politics and ambition of the 'turn': Unpacking the relations between Future 1 and Future 3. *The Curriculum Journal*, 30 (2), 105–124.

Muller, J. and Young, M. (2019). Knowledge, power and powerful knowledge re-visited. *The Curriculum Journal*, 30 (2), 196–214.

Nicolini, D. (2013). *Practice Theory, Work and Organisation: An introduction.* Oxford: Oxford University Press.

Noddings, N. (2003). Is teaching a practice? *Journal of Philosophy of Education*, 37 (2), 241–251.

Nordgren, K. (2017). Powerful knowledge, intercultural learning and history education. *Journal of Curriculum Studies*, 49 (5), 663–682.

Oates, T. (2018). Powerful knowledge – moving us all forwards or backwards? In D. GuileD. Lambert and M.J. Reiss (eds) *Sociology, Curriculum Studies and Professional Knowledge: New perspectives on the work of Michael Young.* London: Routledge, pp. 157–168.

Ofsted (2018). *An Investigation into How to Assess the Quality of Education through Curriculum Intent, Implementation and Impact.* London: Ofsted.

Reiss, M. (2018). The curriculum arguments of Michael Young and John White. In D. GuileD. Lambert and M.J. Reiss (eds) *Sociology, Curriculum Studies and Professional Knowledge: New perspectives on the work of Michael Young.* London: Routledge, pp. 121–131.

Rouse, J. (2007). Social practices and normativity. *Philosophy of the Social Sciences*, 37 (1), 46–56.

Rudolph, S.A. Sriprakash and Gerrard, J. (2018). Knowledge and racial violence: The shine and shadow of 'powerful knowledge'. *Ethics and Education*, 13 (1), 22–38.

Schatzki, T., Knorr Cetina, K. and von Savigny, E. (eds) (2001). *The Practice Turn in Contemporary Theory.* London: Routledge.

Valleriani, M. (2014). Introduction: Appropriation and transformation of ancient science. *Nuncius*, 29 (1), 1–8.

Wheelahan, L. (2015). Not just skills: What a focus on knowledge means for vocational education. *Journal of Curriculum Studies*, 47 (6), 750–762.

White, J. (2018). The weakness of 'powerful knowledge'. *London Review of Education*, 16 (2), 325–335.

Winch, C. (2010). *Dimensions of Expertise: A conceptual exploration of vocational knowledge.* London: Continuum.

Wright Mills, C. (1959). *The Sociological Imagination.* Oxford: Oxford University Press.

Wrigley, T. (2018). 'Knowledge', curriculum and social justice. *The Curriculum Journal*, 29 (1), 4–24.

Yates, L. and Millar, V. (2016). 'Powerful knowledge' curriculum theories and the case of physics. *The Curriculum Journal*, 27 (3), 298–312,

Young, M. (2011). The return to subjects: A sociological perspective on the UK Coalition government's approach to the 14–19 curriculum. *The Curriculum Journal*, 22 (2), 265–278.

Young, M. (2015). Curriculum theory and the question of knowledge: A response to the six papers. *Journal of Curriculum Studies*, 47 (6), 820–837.

Young, M. and Muller, J. (2010). Three educational scenarios for the future: Lessons from the sociology of knowledge. *European Journal of Education*, 45 (1), 11–27.

Young, M. and Muller, J. (2013). On the powers of powerful knowledge. *Review of Education*, 1 (3), 229–250.

Young, M. and Muller, J. (2016). *Curriculum and the Specialisation of Knowledge.* London: Routledge.

Zipin, L, Fataar, A. and Brennan, M. (2015). Can social realism do social justice? Debating the warrants for curriculum knowledge selection. *Education as Change* 19 (2), 9–36.

9

CONCLUDING REMARKS

This final chapter is an opportunity to reflect on the unfolding exploration and subsequent application of the notion of knowledgeable practice, returning in particular to some of the arguments made in the introductory chapter around the rationale for this type of enquiry and addressing some of the implications and questions for further research. While this book has, I hope, made some progress in unpacking some of the tensions in the relation between knowledge and practice in educational studies, there are without doubt further issues that could be potentially discussed in future enquiries.

What has been presented in this book is a conceptualisation of the relation between knowledge and practice that suggests that specialised knowledge requires normative (knowledgeable) practice for its generation, validation and iteration. Shifting somewhat from views of knowledge that concentrate on propositions, concepts or even know-how, the arguments in this book have foregrounded a view of knowledge as closely intertwined with the dynamics of normative practice and notions of mutual accountability, prospectivity and a sense that there must be a shared understanding that there is something 'at stake' if the generation of specialised knowledge and the conditions of the underpinning practice are to be sustained. This is not to say that at any point knowledgeable practice should be seen as coterminous with knowledge. As has been noted in previous chapters (e.g. Chapters 5 and 8, and the example of the recontextualisation of ancient science into the early modern era) it is quite possible for systematic specialised knowledge (which has been made explicit in some form) to exist independently of practice. But it takes certain forms of specialised practice (held within a community of enquirers, perhaps) to recognise the value and relevance of that knowledge, and to systematically revise, recontextualise, apply criteria or standards of excellence, so that knowledge can be dynamically related to that which is 'at stake' in that contemporary practice.

DOI: 10.4324/9781003054474-11

This suggests, perhaps, that there is scope to further develop investigations into the relationship between knowledge and practice in different spheres of education and specific contexts, using the notion of knowledgeable practice as an 'ideal type' or analytical frame from which analysis of a particular scenario can proceed. The notion of knowledgeable practice presented in this book is potentially a helpful model for thinking through how knowledge and practice are presented in education policy, curriculum reform, professional development and in discussions amongst educational practitioners (broadly defined). The notion could be used as a basis for policy scholarship or critique or as part of a comparative study of various types of educational practice.

An issue which a process of conceptual enquiry of this type cannot entirely avoid is the question of boundaries between disciplines or fields of enquiry. In other words, where might this type of enquiry sit in relation to existing educational research? Much of the previous thought that is explored in this book is rooted in the sociology of knowledge and the philosophy of education with some additions from curriculum theory. Educational knowledge and practice are therefore approached from the perspective of some different disciplinary traditions, with the aim of drawing insights from these to address the notion of 'knowledgeable practice' and think through its 'application' to (or consider its implication for) various educational contexts or longstanding educational debates. Inevitably, any reader of this book, drawing on their own disciplinary background, will detect certain research approaches or ways of argument that may or may not be to their liking. However, the overarching aim, as discussed earlier in the rationale, is to attempt to provide a contribution to ongoing debates around the relation between knowledge and practice in education, and this has required an approach that draws from philosophical, sociological and educational sources, while locating the tensions between knowledge and practice in the context of questions of professional education, teaching and curriculum studies.

The research approach taken in the book may also be potentially disorientating for some readers, at least in terms of the methodology of the research employed. As the approach is primarily conceptual and theoretical in orientation, the book does not rely on primary empirical data as such but does contain a number of chapters which seek to engage critically with the contemporary context of policy and representations of practice. Therefore, while there are no interviews or surveys, there have been some illustrations in terms of engagement with documentary sources which provide an outline of the direction of the research field (often influenced by policy) (e.g. Chapter 5) as much as there have been attempts to engage directly with academic debate on notions of knowledge and practice in education (e.g. Chapters 7 or 8). The research approach, if it can be characterised as such, is therefore perhaps illustrative of how the author would see knowledgeable practice *enacted* in educational research, as part of an ongoing prospective disciplinary conversation within a community that has a purpose and a sense that there is something 'at stake'. Rather than seek to sit firmly within a 'sociology of educational knowledge' or 'philosophy of practice' the book therefore perhaps sits at or even between boundaries, seeking to contribute to a more reflective 'educational studies' that recognises the importance of recontextualising or rethinking ideas for the requirements of educational practice in a deliberative fashion, building on some of the arguments that I outline in a recent paper (Hordern 2023).

However, this approach taken in this book also sits across the concerns of various different fields of educational research, aiming to demonstrate how a rethinking of the relation between knowledge and practice in education can help us reconsider various debates in teaching, professional education and curriculum studies – and possibly see some common ground across boundaries. Such an approach also comes with challenges, as the issues considered to be 'at stake' arguably vary across these different fields, and therefore a meaningful contribution requires a sufficient grasp of the relevant debates regarding what is at issue. While in professional or vocational education issues of purpose may be related as much to supporting the development of demonstrable competence or expertise in an occupation, in teaching, curriculum studies or in more general education there may be a greater emphasis on socialisation or on the 'subjectification' that Biesta (2010) discusses. Thus the three immediately preceding chapters of the book (Chapters 6–8) may be judged for their contribution to the 'knowledgeable practice' of professional/vocational education, teaching and curriculum studies by slightly different yardsticks. In each chapter does the approach taken sufficiently grasp widely held notions of what is 'at stake' in these fields of educational enquiry? The approach taken in those chapters has tended to be framed by an engagement with contemporary or recent debates – building on the arguments and postulates of others to provide a critical introduction to issues of concerns within the research community. Inevitably there is more that could be said, and further work to do justice to the issues in each field.

As set out in the rationale earlier in the book, the underpinning research approach is informed by a sense that our notions of 'objectivity' are always shaped by socio-historical conditions and the genealogical development of what counts as 'knowledge'. As noted earlier, this does not discard notions of 'truth' but instead sees such notions as inevitably inflected by the relationship between the social and the epistemic – and this also means acknowledging issues of power and influence over 'what counts' as the established truth. The approach taken in this book is that the primary way to continue our pursuit of the truth and to arrive at fuller understandings of the social world is to further pursue informed discussion and debate, identifying flaws in arguments and attempting to provide better explanations and generate more substantive understandings. If these discussions and debates are undertaken within the context of a knowledgeable practice that recognises that our understandings are always 'prospective' and will always require further deliberation and iteration, then we can maintain reasonable approximations of truth and objectivity that can inform the ongoing development of criteria of excellence which can be used to evaluate aspects of practice. In order to do so, however, there is a continual requirement to maintain the prospectivity *in practice*, and this may entail both a challenge to any stasis or elitism that may develop amongst longstanding expert practice participants, and a requirement to maintain debates about and to be open to potential reconfigurations in our conceptualisations of what is 'at stake' in the practice.

I hope what has been provided as an outcome of the book is a reasonable articulation of a view of the relation between knowledge and practice in education that will have resonance within the discipline or deliberative tradition of 'educational studies' and perhaps specifically in the fields of professional/vocational education, the study of teaching and in curriculum studies. As noted above, it could be argued that the notion of 'knowledgeable practice' developed, relying as it does on a normative notion of practice and a consideration of specialised knowledge and expertise, provides one form of 'ideal type' that might be hard to find in any empirical study. This is not to say that the notion would therefore not be useful – as all forms of 'ideal types' provide helpful templates against which we can check and evaluate existing practice, activity and judgement. However, while the ideal type argument has something to it, it is also important to note that educational ideas have lives of their own, in the sense that ideas can influence thinking about policy and practice in educational contexts. It is therefore possible that notions of knowledgeable practice can become helpful as templates for organising various forms of educational activity. Empirical studies and policy critique, drawing on the notion of knowledgeable practice, can contribute to refining the ideas and demonstrate their utility. Further enquiry and debate, exploring the applicability of the notion, can further contribute to the iteration of the notion itself, providing us all with better and fuller understandings of what might constitute knowledgeable practice in different contexts.

References

Biesta, G. (2010). *Good Education in an Age of Measurement: Ethics, Politics, Democracy*. Boulder, CO: Paradigm.

Hordern, J. (2023). Educational studies and educational practice: A necessary engagement. *British Journal of Educational Studies*, DOI: doi:10.1080/00071005.2023.2213310.

INDEX